清华大学国家"985工程"二期人才培养建设项目资助

当代中国建筑图语

DISCOURSE ON
THE CONTEMPORARY ARCHITECTURE OF CHINA

清华大学建筑学院朱文一工作室

朱文一　ZHU WENYI
陈瑾羲　CHEN JINXI
秦　臻　QIN ZHEN

清 华 大 学 出 版 社
TSINGHUA UNIVERSITY PRESS
北 京

序言

对于中国当代建设状况，
一些惊人的话语在社会上流传：
世界钢铁交易的 25% 是中国人买进的，
全世界 53% 的水泥消耗在中国，
中国的城镇化进程正以每年制造两个波士顿城的速度进行①，
全世界最大的建设工地，
一个随处可见脚手架的国家，
……

从建筑（学）角度来看，
当代中国建筑的境况到底是怎样的？
呈现什么样的发展轨迹？
建设量占世界建筑的比重是多少？
巨大建设量的分布及发展规律如何？
如此大规模建设的规划与设计支撑状况？
建筑媒体的配套程度？
建筑人才的培养状况？
这些问题的答案，
散落于各种书籍报刊文章网络的夹缝中，
以至于建筑师、规划师、景观师等专业人员，
都很难在短时间内获得当代中国建筑的总貌。

本书尝试以数据及事件为线索解读当代中国建筑，
通过创造性的"图语"表达方式汇集以上问题的答案，
整体呈现当代中国建筑状况：

全面——当代中国建筑状况完整版，
通过对 1978—2006 年中国建筑发展轨迹，
中国在世界建筑场中的位置，
中国建设量与法规政策的状况以及设计机构的数量与分布，
中国建筑媒体、竞赛与奖项以及建筑教育等等方面的梳理，
尽可能系统整体地呈现 20 多年来尤其是当下中国建筑的状况。

中立——当代中国建筑状况数据版，
以各种相关数据为基础，
以被全社会公认为选择标准，
以隐形价值判断为导向，
以年度白皮书形式为目标，
尝试建立一个相对客观反映当代中国建筑状况的阅读平台。

直观——当代中国建筑状况图解版，
根据表达内容的不同，
弘扬建筑学专业以图说话的优良传统，
同时考虑读图时代视觉至上的特征，
创造性地编制和绘制各种各样的图表与图解，
探索一种简明呈现建筑现象的表达方法——图语法。

应该说这是一次尚未完成的尝试，
书中内容的涉及面和数据收集以及表达方式等等都有待进一步发掘与提高。
仅以此书抛砖引玉，
与关心当代中国建筑状况的同仁分享，
同时欢迎提出宝贵意见。

朱文一
02/14/2007 于成都和北京

①参见 "读者来信"，《三联生活周刊》2007 年第五期。

PREFACE

Concerning the current construction environment in China,
some astonishing news is spreading around the world:
25% of the world's steel is used by Chinese,
53% of the world's cement consumption is in China,
the speed of urbanization in China is equal to the speed of building two cities the size of Boston in one year[①],
China - the largest construction site of the world,
a country with scaffolds everywhere,
…

From the architectural point of view,
What is the actual situation in contemporary China?
What sort of path of development can be perceived?
What proportion of world construction volume is in China?
How is this massive amount of construction distributed and what is its rule of development?
How do urban planning and design institutions support such a massive construction volume?
How does the architecture media compare?
How does architecture professional training compare?
The answers to these questions,
are scattered in gaps between various books, Journals, articles and information networks,
so that architecture and urban planning professionals,
find it difficult to quickly perceive an overview of the current condition of architecture in China.

This book attempts to interpret Chinese architecture data and events,
with creative "diagraming", to provide the answers to the questions mentioned above,
to express an overall perspective of the current condition of architecture in China as:

General View— a comprehensive version of the current condition of architecture in China,
via sorting the main events of architecture in China from 1978 to 2006,
China's position in world's architecture,
construction volume of China, architecture laws and regulations,
as well as number and distribution of urban planning and design infrastructures,
architecture media, competitions and awards of China, architecture education as well as other aspects,
to present the past 20 years, particularly the current situation of architecture in China as systemically and holistically as possible.

Neutral View— a data version of the current condition of architecture in China,
based on relevant data,
Selected according to society-recognized standards,
guided by intangible value judgement,
proposed as an annually printed white book,
attempting to establish an objective reading platform that reflects the current condition of architecture in China.

Intuitional View— a graphical version of current condition of architecture in China,
according to different expressed context,
to promote the eminent architecture tradition of diagramming instead of using literary prose,
considering the supremacy of visual information processing in an era of pictoral expression,
mapping a variety of graphic charts creatively,
to explore a simple and direct method of expressing architectural phenomenon—the diagramming syntax.

It should be said that this first attempt is a work in progress.
The contents of this book and the collected data and expressions, etc. are subjects to further exploration and improvement.
The book is an appetizer,
meant to be shared with all colleagues interested in the current condition of architecture in China.
All opinions on the subject are welcome and valued.

Zhu Wenyi
Feb.14, 2007, in Chengdu & Beijing

目录

CONTENTS

"中国建筑发展轨迹（1928—2006）"一章主要参考了中国艺术研究院建筑艺术研究所编纂的《中国建筑艺术年鉴》以及邹德侬主编的《中国现代建筑史》等书籍。

The chapter "Major Architecture Events in China (1978—2006)" mainly refers to *Chinese Architecture Art Yearbook* compiled by China Art Research Institute as well as *China Modern Architecture History* edited by Zou Denong and so on.

参考书目
邹德侬.中国现代建筑史—天津.天津：科学技术出版社，2001.5
中国艺术研究院建筑艺术研究所.中国建筑艺术年鉴.北京—北京出版社，2004.3
《人民日报》
《建筑学报》、《世界建筑》、《时代建筑》

0 中国建筑发展轨迹 (1978—2006)
MAJOR ARCHITECTURE EVENTS IN CHINA (1978—2006)

图片来源：陈瑾羲改绘。资料来源：张耀 摄.奥运村工地塔吊最密集
[EB/OL].北京：北京日报,2006(2006-08-02)[2007-02-07].
http://epaper.bjd.com.cn/rb/20060802/200608/t20060802_60226.htm

中国建筑发展轨迹 (1978—2006)

MAJOR ARCHITECTURE EVENTS IN CHINA(1978—2006)

1978—1982 年

1978年
12 月 18 日，党的十一届三中全会在北京举行。中国建筑的发展迎来了新的春天。

1979 年
3 月 12 日，国务院成立国家建筑工程总局和城市建设总局。
8 月，《建筑师》创刊。

1980 年
5 月，中国政府决定在广东深圳、珠海、汕头和福建厦门试办经济特区，此举掀起了中国建筑发展的热潮。
10 月，《世界建筑》创刊。

1982 年
2 月，国务院转批国家建委、国家城建总局、国家文物局《关于保护我国历史文化名城的请示的通知》，"历史文化名城"的概念被正式提出。随后，国务院公布了24 个城市为首批国家历史文化名城。
5 月，国家建委、国家建工总局、国家城建总局、国家环境保护办公室合并，成立城乡建设环境保护部。
10 月，贝聿铭在中国大陆设计的第一个作品——香山饭店建成。这一作品引起了建筑界的广泛关注和讨论。

图 0-1 深圳城市的崛起

1978
Dec. 18, the Third Plenary Session of the 11th Central Committee of the Communist Party (CCP) of China was held in Beijing. China architectural development began to recover.

1979
Mar. 12, the State Council established the General Administration of Construction and the General Administration of Urban Planning.
Aug., the *Architect* Journal began publication.

1980
May, China government decided to set up the special Economic Zone in Shenzhen, Zhuhai, Shantou & Xiamen. This measure created an upsurge in building development in China.
Oct., the *World Architecture* Journal began publication.

1982
Feb., the State Council transferred to approve *Notice of the Request About Protecting Famous Cities of Chinese History and Culture* to the National Construction Commission, the National Urban Construction General Bureau, and the State Cultural Relics Bureau. The concept of "Famous Cities of Chinese History and Culture" was proposed formally. Subsequently, the State Council announced 24 cities as the first batch of famous cities of Chinese history and culture.
May, the National Construction Commission, the State Building Administration, the Urban Construction Administration, and the National Environmental Protection office were amalgamated, and the Ministry of Urban and Rural Construction and Environmental Protection was established.
Oct., the Xiangshan Hotel designed by I. M. Pei as his first building in China mainland was completed. The design aroused widespread attention and discussion.

图 0-2 贝聿铭在大陆的第一个作品——香山饭店

1983 年
7月，中共中央、国务院原则通过批准《北京城市建设总体规划方案》。
11月12日，首都规划建设委员会成立。

1984 年
1月5日，国务院颁发《城市规划条例》。
5月，中国开放沿海14个港口城市。
6月，城乡建设环境保护部正式发出通知，要求设计单位由事业管理改为企业化经营，标志着设计体系逐渐摆脱计划经济的模式。
6月28日，城乡建设环境保护部第一次颁发了年度全国优秀建筑设计获奖名单。

1985 年
1月19日，大地建筑事务所成立，这是中国第一家中外合作经营的建筑设计单位。
8月24日，首都规划建设委员会全体会议通过《北京市区建筑高度方案》。
10月11日，戴念慈设计的阙里宾舍在曲阜落成。该方案引发了建筑界对于如何继承传统形式的争论。
11月8日，中国房地产业协会正式成立。

1983
Jul., the CPC Central Committee, the State Council approved " Beijing City Master Plan" in principle.
Nov.12, the Beijing Municipal Commission of Urban Planning was set up.

1984
Jan. 5, the State Council issued *the Regulations of Urban Planning*.
May, the Chinese Government opened 14 coastal cities.
Jun., the Ministry of Urban and Rural Construction and Environmental Protection informed formally to request the design units to change from enterprise management to commercialized management. It indicated that the design system disposed the planned economy mode gradually.

Jun. 28, the Ministry of Urban and Rural Construction and Environmental Protection awarded the national list of outstanding architectural design in year for the first time.

1985
Jan. 19, the Orient Earth Architecture Company held the inaugural meeting. This was the first design unit of Sinoforeign co-operative joint venture in China.
Aug. 24, the Beijing Municipal Commission of Urban Planning passed *the Program of Beijing Building Height*.
Oct. 11, the Queli Hotel designed by Dai Nianci was completed in Qufu, it aroused dispute among architects about how to inherit the traditional form.
Nov. 8, China Real Estate Association was established.

图 0-2 资料来源：《建筑创作》杂志社编.北京建筑图说 北京 20 世纪的 100 座建筑[M]. 北京: 2004:96-97

中国建筑发展轨迹(1978—2006)
MAJOR ARCHITECTURE EVENTS IN CHINA(1978—2006)

1986—1989 年

1986年

11 月 17 日，全国首次建筑教育思想讨论会在南京召开。

关肇邺教授设计的西单商场方案引起建筑界广泛关注。

1987 年

3 月 25 日，《民用建筑设计通则》颁布，并于同年 10 月 1 日试行。

4 月 10 日，中国建筑业联合会决定从 1987 年起设立建筑工程鲁班奖。

6 月，国家图书馆落成，规模为亚洲同类建筑之首。

7 月 1 日，国家标准《住宅建筑设计规范》颁布实行。

12 月，长城、明清皇宫等 6 处古迹被联合国列入世界文化遗产名录。

1988 年

3 月 28 日，中华人民共和国建设部正式成立。

4 月 28 日，首都 20 万群众投票选出 80 年代十大建筑。

1989 年

3 月，华东建筑设计院设计的上海"东方明珠"电视塔方案经审定作为实施方案。

9 月，吴良镛教授所著《广义建筑学》出版发行。

11 月 17 日，中国风景园林学会成立。

12 月 26 日，《中华人民共和国城市规划法》公布，并于 1990 年 4 月 1 日实施。

图 0-3　中华人民共和国城市规划法颁布

1986

Nov. 17, the seminar about architecture education was held in Nanjing for the first time of China.

Plan of Xidan Mall Design by Prof. Guan Zhaoye caused wide attention in architecture society.

1987

Mar. 25, *Code for Design of Civil Buildings* was issued and implemented on Oct. 1, the same year.

Apr. 10, the China Construction Industry Association (CCIA) decided to set up Luban Prize.

Jun., the National Library of China, the first library of such scale in Asia, was completed in Beijing.

Jul. 1, *Design Code for Residential Buildings* was issued and implemented as national standard.

Dec., six historic sites such as the Great Wall, the imperial palace in the Ming and Qing Dynasties were listed in the United Nations' World Cultural Heritage Registery.

1988

Mar. 28, the Ministry of Construction of P.R.China was formally set up.

Apr. 28, over 200 000 masses in capital Beijing voted and elected ten outstanding buildings of 1980s.

1989

Mar., the scheme of Shanghai television tower "Oriental Pearl" designed by East China Architectural Design & Research Institute Co. Ltd was authorized as the implemented scheme.

Sep., *A General Theory of Architecture* written by Professor Wu Liangyong was published.

Nov. 17, the Chinese Society of Landscape Architects was officially established.

Dec. 26, *City Planning Law of P.R.China* was announced, and officially implemented in Apr. 1, 1990.

图 0-3　资料来源：人民日报[N].1990 年 1 月 4 日第六版，北京

图 0-4　吴良镛设计的菊儿胡同

1990年

4月，中国政府决定开发上海浦东，引发了中国新一轮的建设浪潮。

8月，第一批勘察设计大师名单公布。

9月22日，第十一届亚运会在北京开幕，亚运会促进了北京城市建设的发展。

1991 年

12月27日，全国首届高等学校建筑学专业评估工作会议在南京结束。清华大学、同济大学、天津大学、东南大学四所高校建筑系的建筑学专业获得优秀资格。

1992年

11月20日，上海市政府举办陆家嘴金融贸易中心区规划国际咨询。国内外5家设计单位参加角逐。

1993 年

8月4日，吴良镛、周干峙、林志群合著的报告《我国建设事业的今天和明天》公布。书中首次提出"人居环境学"概念。

10月4日，吴良镛主持设计的菊儿胡同四合院工程被联合国授予"世界人居奖"。

11月6日，中国城市规划学会在襄樊成立。

11

1990

Apr., the Chinese government decided to develop Shanghai's Pudong new district. It set off a new wave of construction.

Aug., the first list of China Exploration & Design Masters was announced.

Sep. 22, the 11th Asian Games was opened. It promoted the development of the city's construction.

1991

Dec. 27, the first working conference of assessment to architecture schools of higher education in China concluded in Nanjing. Tsinghua Univ., Tongji Univ., Tianjin Univ. and Southeast Univ. obtained the outstanding qualification.

1992

Nov. 20, Shanghai government held the international consultation of "Lujiazui CBD Planning". Five domestic and international design units participated in the contention.

1993

Aug. 4, the report *Today and Tomorrow of China Construction* written by Wu Liangyong, Zhou Ganzhi and Lin Zhiqun was announced. It put forward the concept of "Sciences of Human Settlement" for the first time.

Oct. 4, The Ju'er Hutong Quadrangles dsigned by Wu Liangyong, was awarded the title of "The World Habitat Award," in the conference held in the United Nations headquarters.

Nov. 6, the Urban Planning Society of China was established in Xiangfan.

图 0-4　资料来源：楼庆西.凝视 楼庆西建筑摄影集[M].北京,2000：104

中国建筑发展轨迹(1978—2006)
MAJOR ARCHITECTURE EVENTS IN CHINA(1978—2006)

图 0-5　上海浦东的傍晚

资料来源: 秦瑜拍摄于 2004 年 10 月

中国建筑发展轨迹(1978—2006)
MAJOR ARCHITECTURE EVENTS IN CHINA(1978—2006)

1994年
2月17日，国家"安居工程"正式启动，这是为确保到20世纪末实现居住小康目标采取的重大决策。
3月25日，中国政府通过《中国二十一世纪议程——中国二十一世纪人口、环境与发展白皮书》，将可持续发展作为国策。
7月5日，《中华人民共和国城市房地产管理法》正式颁布。
8月，第二批勘察设计大师名单公布。
12月，西藏布达拉宫等4处古迹被联合国列入世界文化遗产名录。

1995 年
9月23日，国务院颁布《中华人民共和国注册建筑师条例》。
11月14日，首次全国一级注册建筑师考试开考，9 100余名考生参加了考试。

1996 年
1月22日，北京西客站落成，成为"夺回古都风貌"运动的顶极之作。其设计引发众多争议。
7月4日，吴良镛获国际建筑师协会评选的建筑评论和建筑教育奖。
11月，96'上海住宅设计国际住宅竞赛揭晓。国内外共100余家设计单位和个人报名参加，递交方案592个，清华大学教师朱文一获得头奖。

图 0-6　全国一级注册建筑师考试大纲

图 0-7　中华人民共和国建筑法颁布

14

1994
Feb. 17, " The Economy Housing Project" officially started. This was to achieve the goal of inhabit well-to-do by the end of the 20th century.
Mar. 25, the Chinese Government approved *China's Agenda 21: White Book on China's Population, Environment and Development in the 21st Century* and regarded sustainable development as state policy.
Jul. 5, *Law of the People's Republic of China on Urban Real Estate Administration* was issued and implemented.
Aug., the second list of Exploration & Design Engineer Masters was announced.
Dec., four historic sites, the Potala Palace, etc., were listed in the United Nations World Cultural Heritage Registery.

1995
Sep. 23, the State Council promulgated *Regulations of P.R. China Registered Architects*.
Nov. 14, more than 9 100 candidates took part in the first registered architects exam in China.

1996
Jan. 22, Beijing West Railway Station was completed. It became a symbol of "neo-classic style" climax, which led to many controversies.
Jul. 4, Wu Liangyong won the Architectural Review and Architectural Education Award by UIA.
Nov., the result of Shanghai International Residential Design Contest'96 was announced. There were more than 100 design units and individuals participating in the competition and 592 designs were submit. Zhu Wenyi, a teacher of Tsinghua University, won the first prize.

图 0-6　资料来源：全国一级注册建筑师考试大纲　中国勘察设计，1995 年第二期
图 0-7　资料来源：人民日报[N]. 1997 年 11 月 4 日第二版，北京

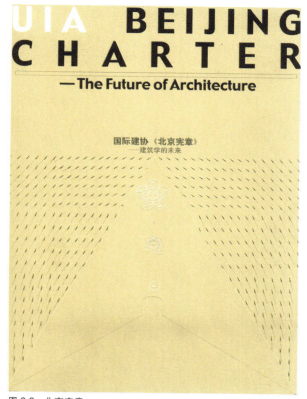

图 0-8 北京宪章

1997 年

3 月 14 日，重庆直辖市成立。此举引发了大规模的城市开发建设。

8 月，东南大学建筑系举行庆祝建系 70 周年纪念活动。

11 月 1 日，国家主席江泽民签署命令，颁布《中华人民共和国建筑法》，1998 年 3 月 1 日起正式实施。

1998 年

7 月 20 日，中国国家大剧院建筑设计竞赛方案在中国国家博物馆公开展出。

10 月 28 日，位于上海浦东的金茂大厦落成，楼高 420m，88 层。高度位居中国当时第一。该项目由美国 SOM 建筑事务所设计。

11 月 3 日，成都市府南河综合整治工程获得了 1998 年度联合国人居奖。

1999 年

5 月 1 日，99' 世界园艺博览会在昆明举行。

6 月 23 日，第 20 届世界建筑师大会在北京召开。来自 100 多个国家和地区的 6 000 多名代表出席会议。围绕 "21 世纪的建筑学" 广泛交流思想，并通过了由清华大学吴良镛教授起草的《北京宪章》。

8 月 30 日，《中华人民共和国招标投标法》获得人大通过，自 2000 年 1 月 1 日起施行。

10 月，为隆重庆祝建国 50 周年，全国各地一大批标志性建筑建成并投入使用。

1997

Mar. 14, Chongqing municipality was established, which triggered a massive urban development.

Aug., the architecture department of Southeast University celebrated its 70th anniversary.

Nov. 1, The Chinese President Jiang Zemin signed *Construction Law of P. R. China*. And then in March 1, 1998, it was officially implemented.

1998

Jul. 20, the architectural design schemes of China National Theater competition were exhibited in National Museum.

Oct. 28, Jinmao Tower located in Shanghai Pudong was completed. The building (420m height, 88 stories) was ranked the tallest in China. This project was designed by SOM Associates, USA.

Nov. 3, Chengdu Funan River Improvement Project obtained the Human Settlements Award of the United Nations in 1998.

1999

May 1, the International Horticulture Exposition '99 was held in Kunming.

Jun. 23, the 20th World Congress of Architects was opened in Beijing. More than 6 000 representatives from over 100 countries and regions attended the meeting. The congress focused on "Architecture in the 21st Century" and passed *Beijing Charter* drafted by Prof. Wu Liangyong.

Aug. 30, the National People's Congress adapted *Law of the People's Republic of China on Tenders and Bid*, and it was implemented on Jan. 1, 2000.

Oct., to celebrate 50th anniversary of founding of P.R. China, a large number of Landmark buildings in China were built.

中国建筑发展轨迹(1978—2006)

MAJOR ARCHITECTURE EVENTS IN CHINA (1978—2006)

2000年

6月，安德鲁国家大剧院方案引起激烈争论。49位两院院士和108名建筑专家上书国务院反对该设计方案，而另外一部分学者则持截然相反的意见。

6月，为适应城市发展的要求，广州市在全国率先开展城市总体发展战略规划研究，确定城市长远发展战略与目标、城市发展方向等重大战略问题。

6月22日，北京颐和园、天坛、重庆大足石刻被列为世界文化遗产。

10月，美国建筑师协会评选20世纪最受欢迎的10座建筑，华裔建筑师林璎的华盛顿越南战争纪念碑和贝聿铭的华盛顿国家美术馆东馆入选。

11月30日，明清皇陵、龙门石窟、都江堰—青城山、皖南古村落—西递、宏村被列入世界文化遗产名录。

12月6日，中国第三批勘察设计大师名单公布。

12月7日，首届"梁思成建筑奖"评选揭晓。

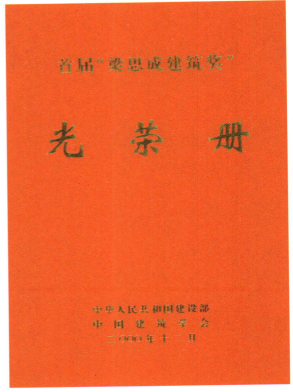

图 0-9　首届梁思成建筑奖光荣册

16

2000

Jun., the Andrews' National Theater design aroused heated debate. 49 academicians and 108 architecture experts sent letters jointly to the State Concil to opppse the scheme strongly. Some other scholars held diametrically opposite opinions.

Jun., in order to adapt urban development, Guangzhou took the lead in China to carry out the city strategy plan research to define great strategy questions such as city long term developmental strategy, urban development direction, etc.

Jun. 22, the Summer Palace, Temple of Heaven and Chongqing's Dazu Stone Carvings were listed as world cultural heritages.

Oct., American Association of Architects selected the 10 most popular 20th century buildings. The Vietnam War Memorial in Washington D.C. designed by Maya Lin and the East Wing of the National Gallery designed by I. M. Pei were on the list.

Nov. 30, Ming and Qing Imperial Mausoleum, the Longmen Grottoes, the Dujiangyan- Qingcheng Moun., Traditional Villages Xidi and Hongcun were included in the World Heritage list.

Dec. 6, the third list of Exploration & Design Engineer Masters was announced.

Dec. 7, the first Liang Sicheng Architecture Award was announced.

图 0-9　资料来源：清华大学建筑学院资料室

图 0-10　世界文化遗产——天坛

秦臻摄于 2007 年 3 月

中国建筑发展轨迹(1978—2006)
MAJOR ARCHITECTURE EVENTS IN CHINA(1978—2006)

2001年

2月，中美签署注册建筑师互认协议。

4月20日，梁思成诞辰100周年纪念会暨《梁思成全集》首发式在北京隆重举行。

4月28日，梁思成先生诞辰100周年纪念会在清华大学举行。

5月15日，20世纪90年代北京十大建筑评选活动揭晓。中央广播电视塔等成为北京"新十大建筑"。

6月，上海里弄旧区改造开发的"新天地"工程竣工。该工程依照"整旧如旧"的思路，较成功地创造出一种旧城改造的开发模式。

7月13日，奥运申办成功。奥运申办成功对北京城市发展具有巨大意义。随之而来的是一大批新型公共建筑的产生和整个北京城市环境的整体提升。

10月18日，由原建设部建筑设计院、中国建筑技术研究院等合并的中国建筑设计研究院正式成立。

10月27日，东南大学隆重纪念杨廷宝诞辰100周年。

11月11日，在世界贸易组织第四届部长级会议上，中国加入世贸组织的申请获得通过。世贸组织的加入对中国建筑发展起到了深远作用。

图 0-11 《梁思成全集》出版

2001

Feb., the Sino-U.S.A. agreement on mutual recognition of registered architects was signed.

Apr. 20, commemorating the 100th anniversary of Liang Sicheng's birth and the celebration ceremony of the first publication of *Complete Works of Liang Sicheng* was held in Beijing.

May 15, the top ten buildings in Beijing of the 1990s were selected. Central TV Tower, etc. become the "top ten new buildings" in Beijing.

Jun. Shanghai's "Xintiandi" project preserving historical "Li-Nong" alleys was completed. Using adaptive reuse and keeping old portions of the city preserved the historic area as a cultural asset in the city.

Jul. 13, the Olympics bid succeeded. The Olympic Games have enormous impact on Beijing city's development. Following the bid announcement, a large construction wave began. The urban environment in Beijing also received intense promotional efforts.

Oct. 18, the former China Building Technology Development Center and the Architecture Design Institute Ministry of Construction were combined to become the China Architecture Design and Research Group(CAG).

Oct. 27, Southeast University sclemnly commemorated the 100th anniversary of Yang Tingbao's birth.

Nov. 11, in the Fourth Ministerial Conference of the World Trade Organization, China's accession to the WTO decision was adopted. WTO accession played a far-reaching role in China's architecture development.

图 0-11 资料来源: 梁思成全集 第七卷 [M].北京: 2001

图 0-12　申奥成功

2002年

1月7日至8日，在全国建设工作会议上，中国首次颁发"中国人居环境奖"和"中国人居环境范例奖"。

5月20日，同济大学建筑学院举行建院五十周年纪念庆祝活动。

7月14日，北京奥林匹克公园和五棵松文化体育中心规划设计竞赛方案评审揭晓。美国 Sasaki Associates，Inc 和天津华汇工程建筑设计有限公司合作的方案获奥林匹克公园规划设计方案一等奖，五棵松文化体育中心一等奖空缺，二等奖两个方案由美国 Sasaki Associates，Inc 和瑞士 Burekhardt－Partner AG 公司获得。

9月8日，在威尼斯双年展第八届国际建筑展上，来自中国的张欣凭"长城脚下的公社"获得"建筑艺术推动大奖"。长城脚下公社是由 12 名亚洲著名建筑师设计的前卫建筑项目。

11月22日，2002 上海双年展开幕，本次双年展的主题是"都市营造"，反映了策划者对都市艺术整体性的关怀。

12月3日，在国际展览局第 132 次大会上，中国上海获得了 2010 年世界博览会举办权，世博会园区建设启动。世博会的申办成功为建筑业带来了新的大发展。

12月，中央电视台新总部大楼设计方案揭晓。荷兰建筑师库哈斯中标，该方案造型奇特、耗资巨大，引起广泛争议。

2002

Jan. 7 to 8, at the National Construction Work Conference, the Award for the "China Human Living Environment" and the Award for the "China Human Living Environment Paradigm" were issued for the first time.

May 20, Architecture School of Tongji University held the celebration of the 50th anniversary of its founding.

Jul. 14, the Beijing Olympic Park and Wukesong Cultural and Sports Center design competition was unveiled. The design by Sasaki Associates and Tianjin Huahui Architectural Design & Engineering Co.Ltd won the first prize. Wukesong Cultural and Sports Center award was vacant. Two second prizes were shared by Sasaki Associates (U.S.A.) and Switzerland Burekhardt-PartnerAG.

Sep. 8, at the 8th International Architecture Exhibition of Venice Biennale, Zhang Xin from China won "Grand Prix for Promoting Architectural Art" according to "the People's Commune at the foot of the Great Wall", which was a fashionable project designed by 12 famous Asian architects.

Nov. 22, the Shanghai Biennale 2002 was opened with the theme "Urban Creation", which reflected sponsor's concern to the urban art.

Dec. 3, at the 132th assembly of the International Exhibition Bureau, Shanghai won the right to host the 2010 World Expo. Successful bid of the Expo brings tremendous business opportunities for construction.

Dec., CCTV's new headquarter's design was unveiled. Dutch architect Rem Koolhaas won the bid. The "Z-shaped" orm aroused widespread controversy.

图 0-12　资料来源：人民日报[N].2001 年 7 月 14 日第一版.北京

中国建筑发展轨迹(1978—2006)
MAJOR ARCHITECTURE EVENTS IN CHINA(1978—2006)

图 0-13 资料来源：周畅主编. 北京宪章在中国 中外建筑师合作设计作品集
1999-2005 [M]北京：中国建筑工业出版社，2005：90
图 0-14 资料来源：周畅主编. 北京宪章在中国 中外建筑师合作设计作品集
1999-2005 [M]北京：中国建筑工业出版社，2005：33
图 0-15 资料来源：美国 Sasaki 设计公司. 通向自然的轴线——北京奥林匹克
森林公园及中心区景观规划设计简介. 建筑学报，2004 (6)

图 0-13

图 0-14   图 0-15

中国建筑发展轨迹(1978—2006)
MAJOR ARCHITECTURE EVENTS IN CHINA(1978—2006)

图 0-16 国家大剧院中标方案

图 0-16、图 0-17 均为秦臻根据以下资料改绘：周畅主编 北京宪章在中国 中外
建筑师合作设计作品集 1999-2005 [M].北京：中国建筑工业出版社，2005：99

图 0-17 中央电视台总部大楼设计方案

中国建筑发展轨迹(1978—2006)
MAJOR ARCHITECTURE EVENTS IN CHINA(1978—2006)

图 0-18 上海 2010 年世博会规划中标方案平面图
图 0-19 上海 2010 年世博会规划中标方案效果图

图 0-18 图 0-19 资料来源：AS. Architecture-Studio 上海 2010 年世博会会
址规划. 世界建筑导报[J].2006.(8)

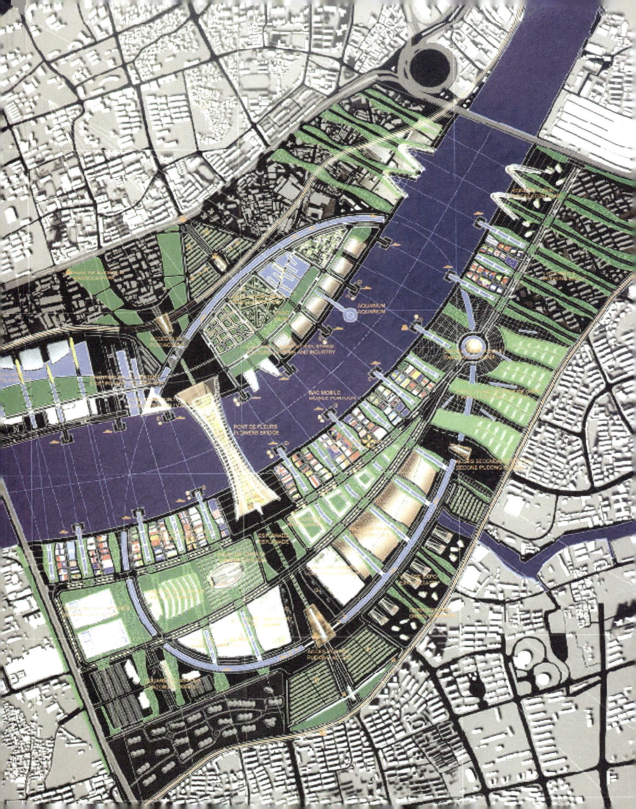

中国建筑发展轨迹(1978—2006)
MAJOR ARCHITECTURE EVENTS IN CHINA(1978—2006)

2003年

1月23日，第二届"梁思成建筑奖"评选揭晓。

2月，全国最大的大学城——广州大学城启动，计划在18km²的岛上修建10所大学，2007年基本建成。

5月14日，卫生部、建设部发布《收治非典型肺炎患者医院建筑设计要则》。传染性"非典"引发整个建筑界对健康建筑设计标准的反思。

6月8日，国家体育场实施方案确定。由瑞士建筑大师赫尔佐格·德梅隆与中国建筑设计研究院联合设计的"鸟巢"方案，确定为实施方案。

9月24日，国家游泳中心设计方案正式确定。由中国建筑工程总公司、澳大利亚PTW公司、澳大利亚ARUP公司组成的联合体设计的"水立方"被确定为实施方案。

10月8日，建设部、国家文物局公布首批中国历史文化名镇、名村，山西省静升镇等10个镇为第一批中国历史文化名镇，北京市爨底下村等12个村为第一批中国历史文化名村。

10月，清华大学建筑学院成立景观系，聘请美国著名景观学家劳瑞·奥林教授为系主任。

图 0-20 "非典"引发建筑界反思

26

2003

Jan. 23, the second "Liang Sicheng Award" was announced.

Feb., the largest university city in China, Guangzhou University City commenced construction. Ten universities are planned on the 18 square kilometers island, scheduled for completion by 2007.

May 14, the Ministry of Health and the Ministry of Construction issued *Typical Pneumonia Patients Admitted to Hospital Architectural Design*. Atypical pneumonia caused reflection on the design standards of healthy building.

Jun. 8, the winning scheme for the National Stadium was chosen: the "Bird Nest" scheme jointly designed by Swiss architect Herzog and De Meuron and the China Architecture Design and Research Group.

Sep. 24, the National Swimming Center design program was officially confirmed. The "Water Cube" scheme designed by China Construction Engineering Corporation, the Australian company PTW and ARUP won the competition.

Oct. 8, the Ministry of Construction and State Administration of Cultural Heritage announced the first Famous Historic Towns and Villages of China. Jingsheng in Shanxi Province and other 9 towns were the first batch of China's famous historic towns, while Cuandixia in Beijing and other 11 villages were the first batch of China's famous historic villages.

Oct., the Landscape Department of Tsinghua Architecture School was founded. The famous American Landscape Architect Laurrie Olin was invited as Department Dean.

图 0-21 中国第一批历史文化名村——周庄

图 0-22 国家图书馆二期方案

10月，首家在中国境内设立的外商独资建筑企业获准成立。

10月22日，中国建筑学会举行成立50周年纪念庆祝活动。中国建筑学会成立于1953年。

10月31日，国家图书馆二期工程暨数字图书馆工程建筑设计方案招标揭晓，德国KSP恩格尔·齐默尔曼建筑设计有限公司和华东建筑设计研究院有限公司联合体的方案被确定为中标方案。

11月，建设部和国家知识产权保护局联合出台《工程勘察设计咨询业知识产权保护与管理导则》。此法规帮助中国工程勘察设计行业在WTO市场环境下，增强知识产权保护意识，提高市场竞争能力。

11月19日，建设部颁发了《关于受理工程勘察、设计企业资质申请等有关问题的通知》。此规定的出台意味着建筑专业设计市场全面放开。

12月10日，广州歌剧院设计选定英国建筑师扎哈·哈迪德的设计方案。

Oct., the first foreign capital architecture enterprise set up in China got permission to be established.

Oct. 22, the Architecture Society of China held the celebration of 50th anniversary of its founding. ASC was founded in 1953.

Oct. 31, the architectural design of the second stage of National Library and the Digital Library were unveiled. The scheme by Germany KSP Engel Zimerman Architectural Design Co., Ltd and East China Architectural Design Research Institute won the bid.

Nov., the Ministry of Construction and National Intellectual Property Protection Office jointly issued *Guide of Exploration and Design Consultation of Intellectual Property Protection and Management in Project*. This regulation helps China's project to review the trade of design under the environment of WTO market, strengthening the consciousness of intellectual property protection and improving the competitive power of market.

Nov. 19, the Ministry of Construction issued *Notice on Accepting the Exploration and Design, Designing Enterprise's Qualification Application*. This regulation opened design market in an all-round way.

Dec. 10, British architect Zaha Hadid won the Guangzhou Opera Theater competition.

图 0-21 秦睢拍摄于 2004 年 3 月
图 0-22 资料来源: 周畅主编. 北京宪章在中国 中外建筑师合作设计作品集 1999-2005. 北京: 中国建筑工业出版社, 2005: 43

中国建筑发展轨迹(1978—2006)
MAJOR ARCHITECTURE EVENTS IN CHINA(1978—2006)

2004 年

4 月 26 日，第四批勘察设计大师名单公布。

6 月 10 日，建设部正式施行《外国企业在中国境内从事建设工程设计活动的管理暂行规定》，明确地规范了外国企业承担中国境内建设工程设计活动的各项行为。同时明确了香港、澳门和台湾地区的设计机构在中国内地从事建设工程设计活动也参照该规定执行。

7 月 7 日，第 28 届世界遗产委员会会议在中国苏州闭幕。大会通过《苏州宣言》，呼吁国际社会和世界各国要更加重视青年人在世界遗产保护中的作用，加强针对青年人的世界遗产保护教育。

7 月 15 日，香港 106 位建筑师与内地 99 名一级注册建筑师成功通过首批互认培训和审核，分别取得内地一级注册建筑师资格和香港建筑师学会会员资格。

8 月 12 日，北京奥组委宣布，2008 年的北京奥运会的场馆建设将进行投资、工期等方面的重新论证，整体完工期将推迟一年。

9 月，《北京城市总体规划(2004—2020)纲要》修编完成。按照新规划，到 2020 年，北京将发展 11 个新城以疏解中心城区压力，总人口控制在 1 800 万人左右，而中心城区则控制在 850 万人以内。

图 0-23　第 28 届世界遗产大会开幕

图 0-24　《北京城市总体规划（2004—2020）纲要》修编完成

2004

Apr. 26, the fourth list of Exploration & Design Engineer Masters was announced.

Jun. 10, the Ministry of Construction implemented *TemPorary Regulation for Foreign Enterprise Engaged in Engineering Design Activity in China*, standardized foreign enterprise to undertake China engineering design in every behavior of activities clearly. Meanwhile the design enterprise in Hong Kong, Macao and Taiwan regions should abide by the regulation in China Mainland at the same time.

Jul. 7, the 28th Meeting of the World Heritage Committee closed in Suzhou. The conference passed *Suzhou Declaration*, calling upon international community to pay more attention to young people's contribution to the world legacy protection and to strenghten youth education on world legacy protection.

Jul. 15, 106 architects of Hong Kong and 99 A-class registered architects in China Mainland succeeded for the first time in reciprocating acceptance of mutual professional training and obtained the inland A-class registered architect's qualification and Hong Kong architect membership, respectively.

Aug. 12, Beijing Olympic Committee announced that, the investment, construction period and some other aspects of Beijing Olympic Stadiums will be rediscussed, the whole completed construction will be delayed for one year.

Sep., the *Guideline Master Plan of Beijing (2004—2020)* was amended and completed. According to new planning, by 2020 Beijing will develop 11 new towns in order to relieve the urban pressure in the center. Total population will be controlled at 18 million and the urban center area population was will be limited to 8.5 million.

图 0-23　资料来源：解放日报. 2004. 6 (2)
图 0-24　资料来源：北京城市规划设计院. 北京城市总体规划(2004—2020 年).
北京规划建设, 2006, (5)

图 0-25　中国台北 101 大楼落成

9月，国家博物馆改扩建工程确定中标方案。建研建筑设计研究院有限公司和德国GMP 国际建筑设计有限公司设计联合体方案中标。

9 月 20 日，首届中国国际建筑艺术双年展在北京人民大会堂开幕。

11 月 8 日，由建筑设计大师程泰宁控股的综合性甲级建筑设计公司开业。这是我国由名人领衔控股设计公司的开始，标志中国民营建筑设计公司进入了一个新的阶段。

11 月 29 日，上海世博会组委会审议并通过了《2010 年上海世博会规划方案》。2010 年上海世博会规划方案经过国际招标，在 10 家国际规划设计公司中选择了三家作为获奖方案，最后的正式方案是集合了 10 家方案的优点重新设计的。

12 月，第三届梁思成奖揭晓。

12 月 31 日，耗时近 7 年，投入营建人力超过 230 万人次的台北 101 大楼落成。该大楼共 101 层，总高度达 508m，被确认为世界第一高楼。

Sep., the scheme designed jointly by Research Institute of the Architectural Design and Germany GMP International Architectural Design Co., Ltd. won the National Museum Extension Project bid.

Sep. 20, the first China International Architecture Biennale was opened in the Great Hall of People in Beijing.

Nov. 8, the A-class architectural design company held by Cheng Taining was opened. This was the beginning of the design companies held by the celebrity. It indicated that the private architectural design companies in China were entering a new stage.

Nov. 29, Shanghai World Expo Organizing Committee reviewed and passed the Expo Program of Shanghai in 2010. Shanghai World Expo Program chose 3 schemes as winners from 10 international design bids. The last formal scheme incorporated aspects from the 10 original schemes.

Dec.,the third batch of Liang Sicheng Award was announced.

Dec. 31, costing nearly 7 years and 2.3 million workers to build, Taibei 101 Tower was completed. The building that amounts to 101 floors and 508 meters total height was confirmed as the tallest building in the world.

图 0-25　资料来源：李祖原建筑事务所 台北 101 大楼设计理念 时代建筑 2005

中国建筑发展轨迹(1978—2006)
MAJOR ARCHITECTURE EVENTS IN CHINA(1978—2006)

2005年

3月5日，温家宝总理提出了要抓好重点行业的节能、节水、节材工作，鼓励发展节能省地型住宅和公共建筑。随后，建设部出台了一系列的规定与通知，建筑行业掀起了倡导节能建筑的热潮。

3月，圆明园未进行建设项目环境影响评价即在湖底铺设防渗膜，此事经媒体披露后，引起轩然大波。

3月26日，国务院办公厅发出《关于切实稳定住房价格的通知》。

4月27日，国务院提出八条措施加强引导调控。

5月11日，建设部等七部委发布了《关于做好稳定住房价格工作的意见》，一系列"房产新政"引发了房地产业的重新洗牌，对建筑设计也产生了重大影响。

6月16日，北京国贸三期工程正式开工，该工程规模为54万m²，包括五星级酒店、高档写字楼、商场电影院等设施。三期全部建成后，北京国贸将成为全球最大的国际贸易中心。

7月1日，中国首部《公共建筑节能设计标准》开始强制实施。该标准标志着中国建筑节能在民用建筑领域全面铺开。

图0-26 "硬撑"

图0-27 "阴阳图纸"大行其道 节能建筑缘何不节能

2005

Mar. 5, Premier Wen Jiabao placed focus in key sectors regarding energy, water and materials saving. He encouraged developing energy and land saving residences and public buildings. Subsequently, the MOC issued a series of regulations and notices, and the construction industry set off a movement to promote energy-saving buildings.

Mar., Yuanmingyuan Park had not carried out an environmental impact assessment study of the construction project before laying an impermeable barrier on the lakebed. This incident caused a great controversy after media revealed.

Mar. 26, the General Office of the State Council issued *Notice on stabilizing Housing Price.*

Apr. 27, the State Council proposed eight principles to strengthen control regulations.

May 11, seven ministries and commissions such as Ministry of Construction released *Opinions on Stabilizing Housing Price* and a series of "New Real Estate Property Policies" to reshuffle the real estate market. These events exerted a great influence on the architectural design.

Jun. 16, the third phase of the Beijing International Trade Center project began construction, the size of this project at 540 000 square meters includes facilities such as a five-star hotel, top-grade office buildings, cinemas and retail markets. The three phases together will become the largest international trade centre in the world.

Jul. 1, the first regulation *Design Standard for Energy Efficiency of Public Buildings* in China began compulsory implementation. This standard marked the energy-saving of building in China fully in operation in civic buildings.

图 0-26　资料来源：冯印澄 绘. 硬撑 [EB/OL]. 新华社 2006.[2007-02-07].
http://news.sina.com.cn/c/p/2005-07-12/22397204386.shtml
图 0-27　资料来源：洛海文. "阴阳图纸"作祟 节能建筑不节能 .[EB/OL] .经济参考报 2006.[2007-02-07].
http://biz.163.com/06/0403/13/2DPMM85O00020QEO.html

图 0-28　上海环球金融中心

图 0-29　中国现存最大的会馆——重庆湖广会馆修复开馆

8 月 15 日，建川博物馆的 8 个抗战分馆落成开放。它由 25 位著名建筑师参与设计的 25 个分馆组成，是中国最大的由民间投资的博物馆群。

9 月 7 日，"150 位中国建筑师在法国"项目最后一批青年建筑师完成了在法国的学业。至此历时 8 年的"150 位中国建筑师在法国"项目圆满结束。

9 月 14 日，我国现存最大的会馆建筑——重庆湖广会馆修复工程完工。这座会馆以禹王宫为中心，包括广东公所、齐安公所等部分组成。是清代"湖广填四川"移民运动的重要见证。

9 月，北京大学建筑学研究中心主任张永和出任美国麻省理工学院(MIT)建筑系主任。这是华裔人士第一次担任美国建筑院系的主任。

11 月 17 日，位于浦东陆家嘴的环球金融中心工程全面启动。建成后的环球金融中心高达 492m，比中国第一高楼金茂大厦高 72m。预计 2008 年竣工。

12 月 10 日，以"城市，开门"为主题的深圳城市建筑双年展开幕。此次展览旨在向观众揭示当代城市发展的现状，强调中国正在发生的有关城市和建筑的文化现象。

Aug. 15, eight branches of the Jianchuan Sino-Japanese War museum were completed. It consists of 25 sub-components designed by 25 well-known architects. it was the largest museum assembly by private investors.

Sep. 7, the last group of young architects in the " 150 Chinese Architects in France" program finished their study in France. This program lasted for eight years with very good results.

Sep. 14, the largest association building in existence in China, Chongqing Huguang Huiguan renovation project, was completed. This project was centred on Yuwang Palace, including Guangdong Gongsuo, Qi An Gongsuo, etc. During the Qing Dynasty, it was the site of important "Huguang to Sichuan" immigrant activity.

Sep., Zhang Yonghe, the director of Beijing University Architecture Center was selected as the department head of Architecture Department in Massachusetts Institute of Technology (MIT). This was the first foreign citizen of chinese origion to serve as a dean in a U.S.A. architecture department.

Nov. 17, the Global Trade Center of Pudong Lujiazui commenced construction. Its height is up to 492 meters, 72 meters higher than Jin Mao Tower, the highest skyscraper in China. It was estimated to be completed in 2008.

Dec. 10, Shenzhen International Urban and Architecture Biennale with the theme of " Opening of the City" commenced. The Biennale introduced to the mainstream society current city development, emphasizing the cultural phenomena of the city and architecture in China.

图 0-28 资料来源：李武英.上海环球金融中心"变脸"记 [J].时代建筑，2006 年第一期

图 0-29 资料来源：周衡义 摄.重庆湖广会馆开馆. [EB/OL]，新华社 2006. [2007-02-07]. http://news.sina. com. cn/c/p/2005-09-29/16557900817.shtml

中国建筑发展轨迹(1978—2006)
MAJOR ARCHITECTURE EVENTS IN CHINA(1978—2006)

2006年

1月21日，《中共中央国务院关于推进社会主义新农村建设的若干意见》正式公布，新农村建设全面展开。

3月1日，《住宅建筑规范》、《住宅性能评定技术标准》实施。《住宅建筑规范》是我国第一部以住宅建筑为一个完整对象，从住宅性能、功能和目标的基本技术要求出发，全文强制的工程建设国家标准。《住宅性能评定技术标准》是我国第一部关于住宅性能评定方法、衡量住宅综合性能水平的推荐性国家标准。

3月，在加拿大多伦多举办的住宅国际竞赛中，来自北京的 MAD 建筑师事务所赢得优胜，这是中国建筑首次通过国际公开竞赛赢得国外超高层建筑的设计权。

5月1日，2006沈阳世界园艺博览会正式开展。

5月29日，建设部等九部委出台《关于调整住房供应结构稳定住房价格的意见》，明确要求新开工商品住房套型建筑面积90m² 以下住房面积所占比重，必须在总面积的70%以上。

6月,北京市规划委员会首次提出《北京四合院建筑要素参考图集》，对四合院的保护和更新将具有重要的参考作用。

6月6日，国务院发布《国务院推进天津滨海新区开发开放有关问题的意见》。从地方战略上升到国家战略，天津滨海新区由此展开了大规模建设。

图 0-30　天津滨海新区鸟瞰

2006

Jan. 21, *Opinions on Advancing New Socialistic Rural Construction by the State Council of Central Committee of the Communist Party in China* was announced, and the new rural construction was launched.

Mar. 1, *Residential Building Code* and *Standard for Performance Assessment of Residential Buildings* were implemented. *Residential Building Code* is the first standard in China, developed solely for residential architecture: this compulsory engineering construction national standard is based on functional, performance-related and basic technical requirements of residential housing. *Standard for Performance Assessment of Residential Buildings* is the first in China to recommend national standard that evaluates the method of measuring the comprehensive performance level of housing.

Mar., MAD Architect Associates from Beijing won theInternational Housing Competition held in Toronto, Canada. It was the first time a Chinese architect won an international skyscraper design competition.

May 1, The International Horticulture Expo. 2006 hosted by Shenyang was launched.

May 29, nine ministries and commissions such as the Ministry of Construction issued *Suggestion on Adjusting the Housing Supply Structure to Stabilize the Housing Price*. It required more than 70% of new housing construction maintain below 90 square meters of architectural area.

Jun., Beijing Planning Committee proposed for the first time *The Consultation Collection of Key Elements of Beijing Quadrangles*. It will be an important reference for the protection and renewal of Quadrangles.

Jun. 6, the State Council announced *Opinion on Advancing the Tianjin Binhai New Area Development*, meaning that local strategy has risen to a national strategy. Consequently, the Tianjin Binhai New Area entered a stage of massive coustruction.

图 0-30 资料来源：张建平. 中国重大金融改革将安排在滨海新区先行先试.
[EB/OL], 新华社 9 月 11 日电 2006.[2007-02-07].
http://business.sohu.com/20060912/n245291870.shtml

图 0-31　亚建协大会在北京召开

图 0-32　贝聿铭设计的苏州博物馆落成

6月1日,《绿色建筑评价标准》实施,这是我国第一部从住宅和公共建筑全寿命周期出发,多目标、多层次对绿色建筑进行综合性评价的推荐性国家标准。

8月,2010年上海世博会园区开工。

9月19日,第12届亚洲建筑大会在北京隆重开幕。大会围绕"演变中的亚洲城市与建筑"这一主题,共同讨论国际建筑交流与亚洲的机遇、建筑的可持续发展与新技术、新材料等议题内容。

10月6日,世界著名建筑大师贝聿铭设计的苏州博物馆新馆正式开馆。贝聿铭亲自为博物馆揭幕。由于新馆位置紧邻拙政园,其建筑形式引发争议。

10月21日,清华大学建筑学院举行建院六十周年纪念庆祝活动。

10月21日,清华大学公布了由两院院士吴良镛主持的"京津冀地区城乡空间发展规划研究"二期报告,提出"首都地区"概念,认为京津冀地区城乡空间发展应该构建"一轴三带"。

12月20日,马清运出任美国南加州大学建筑学院院长就职仪式在上海举行。这是华人建筑师第一次在美国高校获此殊荣。

12月27日,中国第五批勘察设计大师名单公布。

Jun．1, *Valuation Standard for Green Building* was implemented. It is the first national standard based on an understanding of residential and public building life-cycles to develop a multiple-goaled and many-leveled comprehensive evaluation of green architecture.

Aug., Shanghai World Exposition 2010 garden came into operation.

Sep. 19, the 12th World Congress of Asian Architects was opened in Beijing with the conference theme "Developing Cities and Buildings in Asia". Architects discussed topics such as international communications, opportunities in Asian architecture, sustainable development, new building materials and new building technology.

Oct. 6, the Suzhou Museum, designed by the famous architect I.M. Pei, was officially opened. Mr. Pei attended the museum opening. The architecture form aroused controversy due to its location close to Zhuozhengyuan Garden.

Oct. 21, the Architecture School of Tsinghua University celebrated the 60th anniversary of the founding.

Oct. 21, Tsinghua University released the report " Research on the Rural & Urban Spatial Development Planning for Beijing, Tianjin and Hebei Province (second phase)" written by academician, Wu Liangyong. The report set the concept "The Capital Region", suggesting that the Beijing-Tianjin - Hebei region's urban and rural development should utilize an "Axis of Tri-bands."

Dec. 20, the inauguration ceremony that Ma Qingyun was appointed the dean of Architecture School in the University of Southern California was held in Shanghai. This was the first time that a Chinese architect received Such a position in an American university.

Dec. 27, the fifth batch of Exploration & Design Master was announced.

图 0-31 资料来源:李丁 第十二届亚洲建筑师大会开幕式主席发言 .[EB/OL],中国建筑学会, 2006.[2007-02-07].
http://member.chinaasc.org/?action_viewnews_itemid_313
图 0-32 资料来源:邱勇 摄 苏州博物馆新馆中秋节开馆 贝聿铭大师亲自揭幕.[EB/OL] ,新华社 9 月 19 日电 2006. [2007-02-07].http://news.xinhuanet.com/politics/2006-10/07/content_5172466.htm

图片来源：陈瑶截改绘。资料来源：张耀 摄.奥运村工地塔吊量征集.
[EB/OL].北京：北京日报,2006[2006-08-02].
[2007-02-07].http://epaper.bjd.com.cn/rb/20060802/200608/t20060802_60226.htm.

1 中国与世界建筑
CHINA`S POSITION IN WORLD`S ARCHITECTURE

十五国建设市场风险和机遇

MARKET POTENTIAL AND OPPORTUNITY VERSUS RISK OF 15 COUNTRIES

建筑市场潜力——机遇与风险
MARKET POTENTIAL– OPPORTUNITY VERSUS RISK
建设风险评分（按5年计算）　圆圈直径大小=全年建设开销（2004 年）

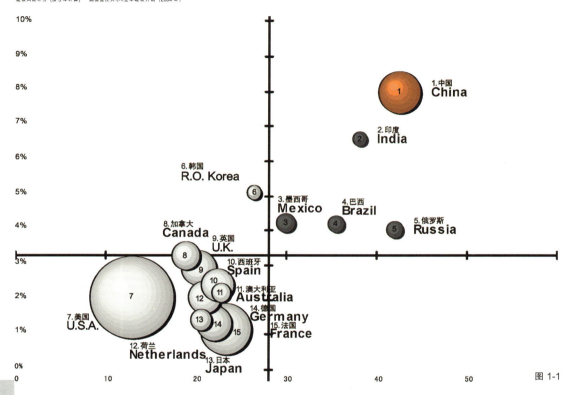

图 1-1

根据全球建设展望组织的统计，中国是2004 年世界上最具活力的建筑市场，同时，这个巨大的市场也容纳最大程度的不安定因素。机遇与风险并存，是中国当代的现状。印度的机遇与挑战仅次于中国，居于第二位。相比之下，韩国是世界上同时具有潜力和投资保障的建筑市场。

According to the statistics of Global Construction Outlook, China is the most active construction market in the world in 2004. At the same time, the huge market accommodates many uncertain factors. Opportunities coexist with risks. It is also the contemporary situation of China. Abundant opportunities and risks also exist in India, second only to China. In comparison, R.O. Korea appears to be the top country when weighing both potential and investment stability.

图 1-1 来源：金秋野根据以下资料改绘.图片来源 Global Construction Outlook 2005 [EB/OL]，Global Insight，Inc. [2007-02-04].http://www.globalinsight. com/gcpath/GlobalConstruction-Brochure.pdf.
注：Compound Annual Growth Rate (CAGR)为复合年均增长率，一项投资在特定时期内的年度增长率计算方法为总增长率百分比的 n 方根，n 相等于有关时期内的年数。

七国建筑价值
VALUE OF BUILDINGS OF 7 COUNTRIES

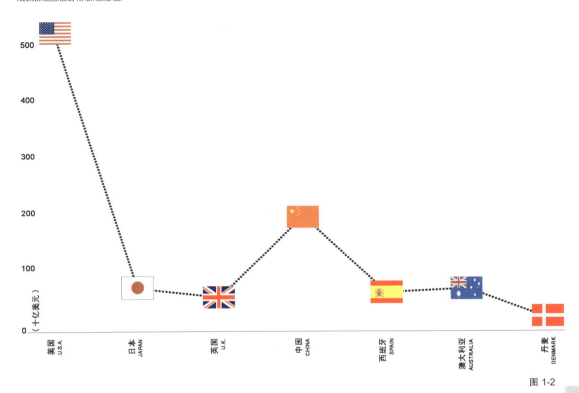

图 1-2

According to the Statistical Yearbook and relative data from seven countries, in measuring the total value of building construction in 2002, the U.S.A. took the first place. China took the second place, a large gap behind the U.S.A.. Japan, the U.K., Spain and Australia share the relatively same value, about half of China's.

根据各国统计年鉴和相关统计数据整理，2002 年，在 7 国房屋建筑总价值中，美国高居首位，中国位于第二位，但是与美国的差距较大，约相当于美国的 2/5。日本、英国、西班牙和澳大利亚等国建筑总价值基本相当。每个国家的建筑总价值约为中国的 1/2。

图 1-2 来源：陈瑾羲根据以下资料绘制。中国数据来自 15-9 各地区建筑业总产值（2004 年），2005 中国国家统计年鉴[M]；
丹麦数据来自 TABLE:CONSTRUCTION OUTLOOK SUMMARY,GLOBAL CONSTRUCTION 2005[EB/OL],GLOBAL INSIGHT；
美国数据来自 Table 927. Construction--Establishments,Employees,Payroll ,Value of Construction, Costs, and Capital Expenditures by Kind of Business (NAICS Basis)[EB/OL]: 2002；
英国数据来自 Table 1.1 New orders obtained by contractors,CONSTRU-CTION STATISTICS ANNUAL 2005[EB/OL],UK；
日本数据来自 TABLE9-2 VALUE OF CONSTRUCTION ORDERSRECEIVED BY KIND OF CONSTRUCTION (F.Y. 1990~2003)[EB/OL],日本统计年鉴，日本国家统计局，2005；
澳大利亚数据来自 HTTP://WWW.CFC.ACIF.COM.AU/，construction frocasting council（CFC)[EB/OL]，AUSTRALIA,2005；
西班牙数据来自《2002 年建设部赴英国、西班牙、法国关于建筑师执业资格制度的考察报告》[EB/OL],建设部中国工程信息网。

十一国注册建筑师数量
NUMBER OF REGISTERED ARCHITECTS OF 11 COUNTRIES

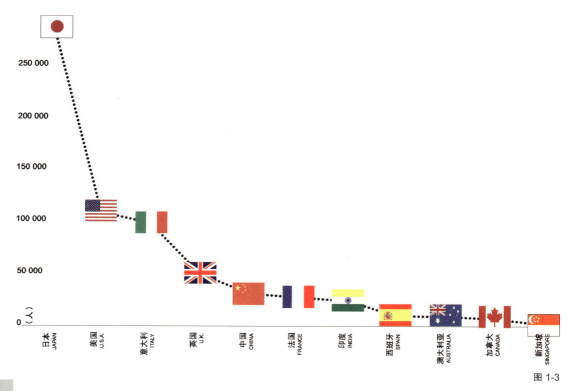

图 1-3

38

根据对 *The Phaidon Atlas Contemporary World Architecture* 书中资料的整理，2000 年在 11 国的建筑师数量排位中，中国排在第 5 位，日本、美国、意大利、英国分别排在前四位。

中国目前注册建筑师总人数(包括一级、二级)约 30 000 人，约为日本的 1/10,约是美国的 1/4,和法国、印度的数量基本持平。

According to *The Phaidon Atlas Contemporary World Architecture* 's data of the number of registered architects in 11 countries in 2000, China ranked the fifth, while Japan, U.S.A., Italy and U.K. took the top four.

China' s current total number of registered architects (including A-class and B-class) is around 30 000, about 1/10 of Japan's, about 1/4 of the U.S.A.'.s, and almost equal to the number of France or India.

图 1-3 来源: 陈瑾羲根据以下资料绘制.数据来源: 《The Phaidon Atlas Contemporary World Architecture》[M].美国:Phaidon,2005:14-15

十一国每百万人注册建筑师数量
NUMBER OF REGISTERED ARCHITECTS PER MILLION PEOPLE OF 11 COUNTRIES

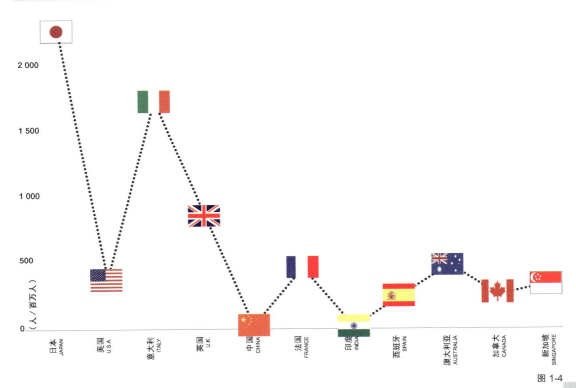

图 1-4

According to the information collected from *The Phaidon Atlas Contemporary World Architecture*, the analysis of the number of registered architects per million people of 11 countries in 2000 revealed that, Japan, Italy, U.K., France and Australia took the top five.

China ranks at a rearward position only higher than India, because of China's large population. Respectively, Japan or Italy has a very large number of registered architects per million people, about 100 times the number in China.

根据对 *The Phaidon Atlas Contemporary World Architecture* 书中资料的整理，2000 年在 11 国的每百万人建筑师数量排位中，日本、意大利、英国、法国、澳大利亚分别排在前 5 位。

中国排在较靠后的位置。中国人口众多，每百万人的注册建筑师数量仅高于印度，而人均注册建筑师最多的是日本和意大利，约是中国每百万人建筑师数量的 100 倍。

图 1-4 来源：陈瑾羲根据以下资料绘制.数据来源：《The Phaidon Atlas Contemporary World Architecture》[M].美国:Phaidon.2005:14-15;
各国人口资料来源世界各国人口统计数据[EB/OL].百度知道，[2007-02-15].
http://zhidao.baidu.com/question/14615941.html?md=3

七国建筑院校数量
NUMBER OF ARCHITECTURE SCHOOL OF 7 COUNTRIES

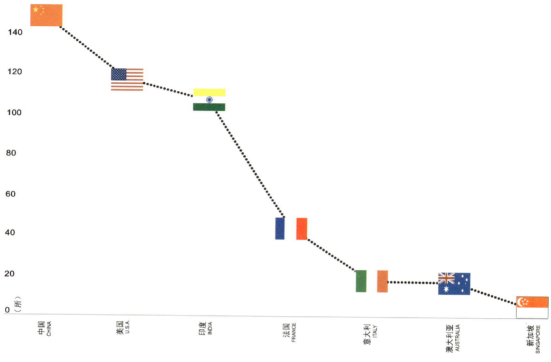

图 1-5

40

根据 *The Phaidon Atlas Contemporary World Architecture* 中数据统计，2000 年在各国建筑院校数量的排位中，中国名列第一，和美国、印度分列前三位，这 3 个国家和其他国家比较优势较大。

中国目前大约有 170 余所建筑院校，20 世纪 90 年代中后期至今数量迅猛增长。美国和印度的建筑院校也超过了 100 所。

According to data collected from *The Phaidon Atlas Contemporary World Architecture*, the analysis of the number of architecture schools of seven countries in 2000 reveals that China, ranked the first, and along with the U.S.A. and India, took the top three positions. The top three were ahead of the other countries by a large margin.

China currently has more than 170 architecture schools, with the number having rapidly increased during the mid-to-late 1990s. The U.S.A. and India both have more than 100 architecture schools.

图 1-5 来源：陈璟羲根据以下资料绘制.数据来源：中国院校数量根据网站不完全统计；其他国家院校数量:The Phaidon Atlas Contemporary World Architecture[M].美国:Phaidon.2005:14-15

按照建筑院校数量排序
RANKING ACCORDING TO NUMBER OF ARCHITECTURE SCHOOLS

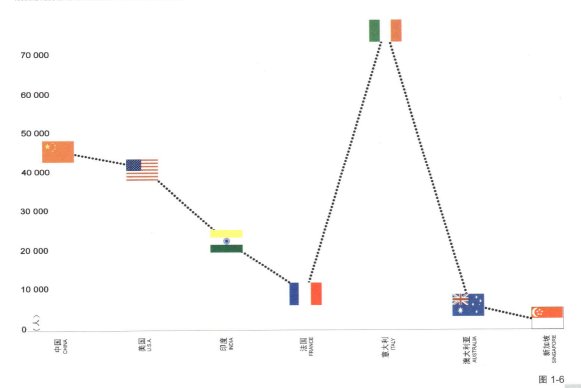

图 1-6

41

According to data revealed in *The Phaidon Atlas Contemporary World Architecture*, an analysis of the number of architecture students showed that, in 2000, Italy placed first, joined by China, the U.S.A. and India to make the top four. The top four were ahead by a large margin.

根据 *The Phaidon Atlas Contemporary World Architecture* 中数据统计，2000 年在各国建筑专业学生数量的排位中，意大利名列第一，中国、美国和印度分列二、三、四位，它们与其他国家相比具有较大的优势。

图 1-6 来源：陈瑾羲根据以下资料绘制.数据来源：中国学生数量根据网站不完全统计；其他国家学生数量：The Phaidon Atlas Contemporary World Architecture[M].美国:Phaidon.2005:14-15

各国人口资料来源世界各国人口统计数据[EB/OL],百度知道，[2007-02-15]. http://zhidao.baidu.com/question/14615941.html?md=3

世界 300m 以上超高层建筑分布
DISTRIBUTION OF SKYSCRAPERS OVER 300 METERS (INCLUDING TOWERS)

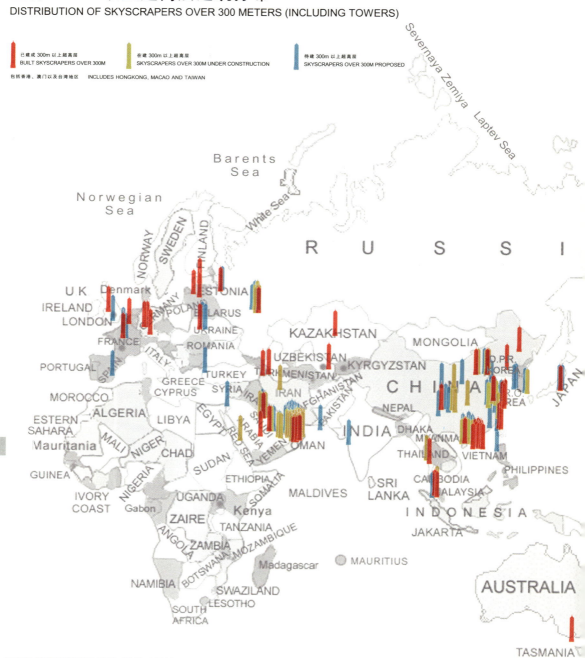

已建成 300m 以上超高层
BUILT SKYSCRAPERS OVER 300M

在建 300m 以上超高层
SKYSCRAPERS OVER 300M UNDER CONSTRUCTION

待建 300m 以上超高层
SKYSCRAPERS OVER 300M PROPOSED

包括香港、澳门以及台湾地区   INCLUDES HONGKONG, MACAO AND TAIWAN

图 1-7 来源：陈瑾羲根据以下资料绘制.数据来源：世界 300m 以上的超高层
建筑[EB/OL].美国：skyscraperpage.com 协会，2007[2007-02-06].http://
skyscraperpage.com；底图来源：http://www.phnx-international.
com/Pictures/Photogallery%20-%20Job%20Locations/World%20Map%
20with%20Job%20Locations%204x2%204-15-2005.jpg

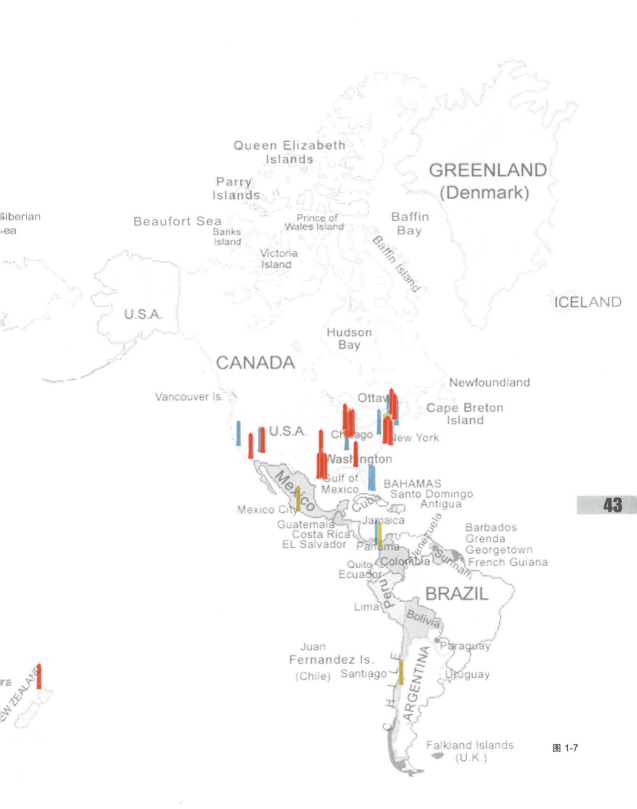

Siberian
ea

Beaufort Sea

Queen Elizabeth
Islands

Parry
Islands

Prince of
Wales Island

Banks
Island

Victoria
Island

GREENLAND
(Denmark)

Baffin
Bay

Baffin Island

ICELAND

U.S.A.

Hudson
Bay

CANADA

Vancouver Is.

Newfoundland

Ottaw

Cape Breton
Island

U.S.A.

Chicago

New York

Washington

Gulf of
Mexico

Mexico

BAHAMAS
Santo Domingo
Antigua

Mexico City

Cuba

Guatemala
Costa Rica
EL Salvador

Jamaica

Panama

Venezuela

Colombia

Surinam

Barbados
Grenda
Georgetown
French Guiana

Quito
Ecuador

Peru

BRAZIL

Lima

Bolivia

Juan
Fernandez Is.
(Chile)

Santiago

Paraguay

CHILE

ARGENTINA

Uruguay

NEW ZEALAND

Falkland Islands
(U.K.)

43

图 1-7

300m 以上超高层建筑中的中国超高层建筑

CHINA'S SKYSCRAPERS OVER 300 METERS AMONG THE WORLD

包括香港、澳门以及台湾地区　INCLUDES HONGKONG，MACAO AND TAIWAN

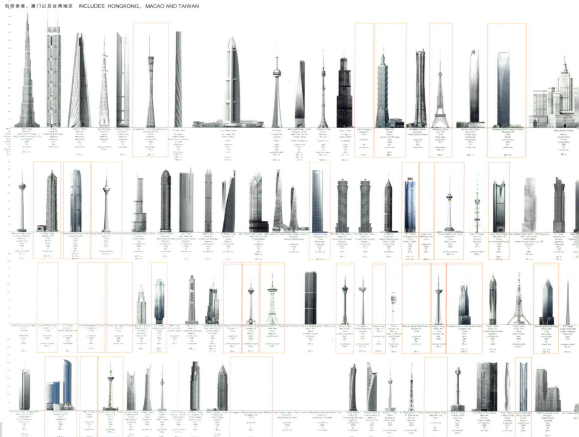

根据 skyscraperpage.com 网站数据统计，截至 2007 年 2 月 2 日，全世界 300m 以上的超高层建筑（高楼和塔）有 196 座。其中 69 座建成，在建 61 座，计划待建 66 座。不同类型中，摩天大楼 152 座，观光塔、通讯塔等共 44 座。

已建成的 69 座超过 300m 的超高层（高楼和塔）中，中国共有 20 座，排在第一位，美国 16 座，排在第二。中国和美国两国的已建成 300m 以上超高层数量约占全世界总数的 52%。澳大利亚、德国、马来西亚和阿拉伯联合酋长国各有 3 座，并列第三位。按照屋顶高度统计，中国台北 101 大厦位列第一，为 448m。按照总高度统计，101 大厦排列第四，为 508m。

According to skyscraperpage.com, by Feb. 2, 2007, there were a total of 196 skyscrapers (high-rises and towers) over 300 meters. Of the 196, 69 are built, 61 are under construction while 66 are proposed. 152 are high-rises and 44 are towers.

Among the 69 built skyscrapers (high-rises and towers) over 300 meters, China has the largest number, at 20, the U.S.A. takes the second, at 16. The sum of the two countries made up 52% of the world. Australia, Germany, Malaysia and the United Arab Emirates possessed 3 each, tying for third. According to the roof height, China Taipei 101 Building ranked the 1st with 448 meters. While according to the total height, 101 building takes the 4th with 508 meters.

Among all the built, under-construction and proposed skyscrapers (high-rises and towers) over 300 meter, ranked according to total height, Burj Dubai in the United Arab Emirates will take the 1st place with a spire height of 807.7 meters, Guangzhou TV Tower will take the 6th place with a total height of 610 meters. According to total number of skyscrapers, China will take the 1st place with 55 buildings, which is about 28% of the world total. The United Arab Emirates ranked the 2nd, with 40 or 20% of the world total; The United States ranked the 3rd, with a total of 32, about 16% of the world total.

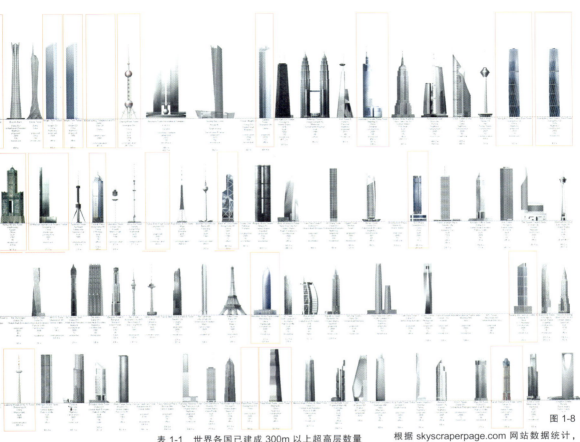

图 1-8

表 1-1 世界各国已建成 300m 以上超高层数量

Country	Number of Built Building over 300 Meters	Country	Number of Built Building over 300 Meters
China	20	Lithuania	1
U.S.A.	16	New Zealand	1
Australia	3	Qatar	1
Germany	3	Saudi Arabia	1
Malaysia	3	Thailand	1
United Arab Emirates	3	Ukraine	1
Canada	2	U.K.	1
Russia	2	Uzbekistan	1
Armenia	1		
Azerbaijan	1		
Belgium	1		
Estonia	1		
France	1		
Japan	1		
Kazakhstan	1		
Kuwait	1		
Latvia	1		

中国，29%

其他国家，48%

美国，23%

图 1-9 已建成 300m 以上超高层比例

根据 skyscraperpage.com 网站数据统计，截至 2007 年 2 月 2 日，全世界目前世界上所有待建、在建和建成的超高层（高楼和塔）中，按照总高度排序，阿拉伯联合酋长国 Burj Dubai 以 807.7m 排在首位。中国广州电视观光塔将位列第六，高度为 610m。在数量上，中国排位第一，有 55 座，约占总数的 28%。阿拉伯联合酋长国位列第二，有 40 座，约占 20%。美国位列第三，共 32 座，约占 16%。

图 1-8 来源：陈瑾根据以下资料改绘.数据来源：世界 300m 以上的超高层建筑[EB/OL].美国：skyscraperpage 协会, 2007[2007-02-06].http://skyscraperpage.com.

表 1-1 来源：陈瑾根据以下资料绘制.数据来源：世界 300m 以上的超高层建筑[EB/OL].美国：skyscraperpage 协会, 2007[2007-02-06].http://skyscraperpage.com.

图 1-9 来源：陈瑾根据表 1-1 数据绘制

2 中国建设量与法规
CONSTRUCTION STATISTICS OF CHINA

1995—2005 年中国全社会年建设规模变化
CHANGE OF TOTAL SIZE OF YEARLY CONSTRUCTION IN CHINA, FROM 1995 TO 2005

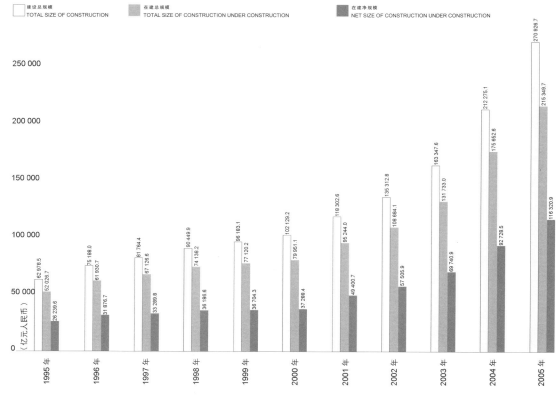

建设总规模
TOTAL SIZE OF CONSTRUCTION

在建总规模
TOTAL SIZE OF CONSTRUCTION UNDER CONSTRUCTION

在建净规模
NET SIZE OF CONSTRUCTION UNDER CONSTRUCTION

图 2-1

48

1995年以来，全社会建设量发生了巨大的变化。全社会建设总规模从 1995 年的 62 978.54 亿元增长到了 2005 年的 270 926.7192 亿元，是 1995 年的 3 倍多。2000—2005 年的增长速度比 1995—2000 年更为迅速。

Since 1995, China's construction of the whole society has undergone tremendous changes. The overall construction size has grown from 6 297.854 billion Yuan in 1995 to 27 092.67192 billion Yuan in 2005, more than three times that of 1995. The speed of expansion from 2000 to 2005 is even faster than that between 1995 to 2000.

图 2-1 来源：陈璟蠹根据以下资料绘制：表 6-8 各地区全社会建设总规模[M].// 中华人民共和国国家统计局 编.2006 中国统计年鉴.第一版.北京：中国统计出版社，2006:616

1 : 2 : 9

1985

建筑业房屋竣工面积 17 072.7 万 m²，
施工面积 35 491.8 万 m²

1995

建筑业房屋竣工面积 32 393.3 万 m²，
施工面积 89 862.8 万 m²

2005

建筑业房屋竣工面积 159 406.2 万 m²，
施工面积 352 744.7 万 m²

图 2-2

49

Building floor space completed yearly increased rapidly: 170.727 million square meters in 1985, 323.933 million square meters in 1995 (almost 2 times more than 1985), and 1 594.062 million square meters in 2005 (nearly 5 times more than 1995 or 9 times more than 1985).

Buildings floor space under construction also increased incredibly, from 354.918 million square meters in 1985 to 898.628 million square meters in 1995 (almost doubled), and up to 3 527.447 million square meters in 2005 (almost 10 times than 1985). Building floor space under construction is growing faster than building floor space completed.

建筑业房屋年竣工面积增长迅速，1985 年为 17 072.7 万 m²，1995 年则为 32 393.3 万 m²，是 1985 年的近两倍；而 2005 年的建筑业房屋竣工面积则为 159 406.2 万 m²，是 1995 年的近 5 倍，是 1985 年的 9 倍多。

建筑业房屋施工面积也有大幅度增长，从 1985 年的 35 491.8 万 m² 增加到 1995 年的 89 862.8 万 m²，翻了一番多，2005 年则高达 352 744.7 万 m²，是 1985 年的近 10 倍。建筑业房屋施工面积的增长速度大于房屋竣工面积的增长速度。

图 2-2 来源：金秋野根据以下资料绘制.数据来源：表 15-37 建筑业房屋建筑面积[M].// 中华人民共和国国家统计局 编 2006 中国统计年鉴.第一版.北京：中国统计出版社，2006:616；图片来源：[瑞士]W·博奥席耶 编著.模度，人类一种新的度量标准：勒·柯布西耶全集.[M].牛燕芳 程超 译.北京：中国建筑工业出版社，2005: 164

1985—2005 年中国房屋建筑总面积变化

CHANGE OF YEARLY FLOOR SPACE OF BUILDINGS OF CHINA, FROM 1985 TO 2005

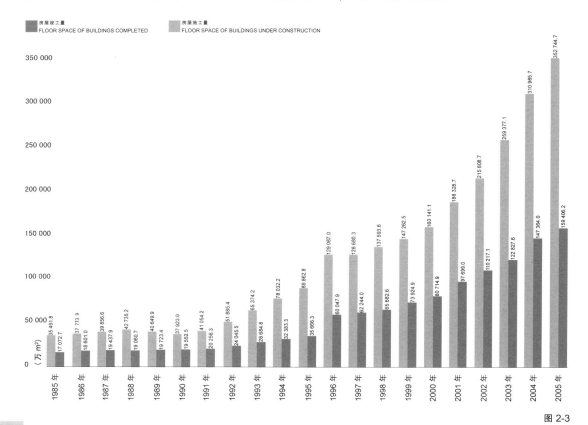

图 2-3

1985年以来，中国房屋建筑年度施工、竣工面积发生了巨大变化。从房屋建筑年度竣工面积来看，可以划分为三个阶段。

第一个阶段是 1985—1991 年，房屋建筑年度竣工面积变化较小，1989—1991 年间甚至出现小幅回落。

第二个阶段是 1992—1995 年的稳步增长，以每年约为前一年竣工面积 14%的速度递增。

第三个阶段是 1996 年至今的快速增长。1996 年度房屋竣工面积较 1995 年增加了68%。1996—2000 年的增长速度稍有下降，平均增幅约为前一年竣工面积的 7%。2000—2005 年，房屋建筑年度竣工面积增长速度上升，平均增幅较为一致，约为前一年竣工面积的 14.7%。

Since 1985, China's annual building floor space data has undergone tremendous changes. Regarding building floor space completed, three stages can be divided.

In the first stage (1985—1991), annual building floor space completed did not change much. A slight decline even happened from 1989 to 1991.

In the second stage (1992—1995) annual building floor space completed increased 14% from the previous year.

The third stage (1996—) is characterized by rapid growth. The building floor space completed in 1996 increased about 68% from 1995. From 1996 to 2000, the growing speed decreased slightly, with an average rate of 7% of previous year. From 2000 to 2005, the growing speed increased to the average rate of 14.7%.

图 2-3 来源：金秋野根据以下资料绘制.数据来源：表 15-37 建筑业房屋建筑面积[M].// 中华人民共和国国家统计局 编.2006 中国统计年鉴.第一版.北京：中国统计出版社，2006:616

1985—2005 年中国国有房屋建筑面积变化

CHANGE OF YEARLY STATE-OWNED FLOOR SPACE OF BUILDINGS OF CHINA, FROM 1985 TO 2005

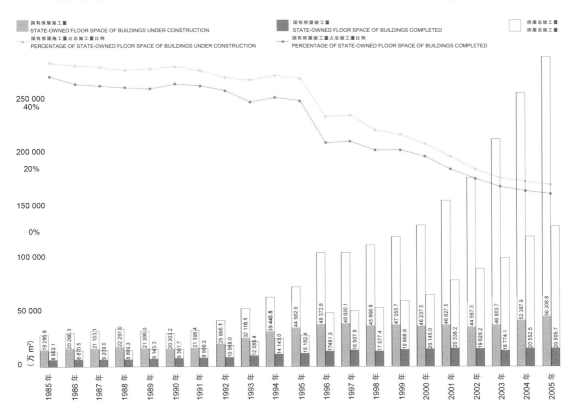

图 2-4

According to the annual building floor space completed, from 1985 to 1991, China's state-owned annual building floor space completed is about 47% of the total amount. From 1992 to 1995, the state-owned proportion declined slightly, to 43%. While in 1996, the proportion decreased rapidly from 42% to 29%. Since then, the state-owned annual building floor space completed declined overall to 13% in 2005, with a decreasing tendency in the near future.

Proportion of China's state-owned annual building floor space under construction is a little bit higher than state-owned annual building floor space completed, about 54% in 1985, while only 16% in 2005.

从房屋建筑年度竣工面积来看，1985—1991 年，我国国有房屋建筑面积在总建筑面积中的比例约为 47％。1992—1995，国有房屋建筑所占比例略有下降，约为 43％。1996 年国有房屋建筑面积占总建筑面积的比例骤然下降，从 1995 年的 42％下降到 29％。自 1996 年开始，国有房屋建筑占总建筑面积的比例整体滑坡，从 1996 年的 29％下降到 2005 年的 13％，且呈现出进一步下滑的趋势。

从房屋建筑年度施工面积来看，国有房屋建筑施工面积占总建筑施工面积的比例则略高于竣工面积。1985 年约为 54％，2005 年则仅为 16％。

图 2-4 来源：金秋野根据以下资料绘制.数据来源：表 15-37 建筑业房屋建筑面积[M]// 中华人民共和国国家统计局 编.2006 中国统计年鉴.第一版.北京：中国统计出版社,2006:616

1995年中国各省、市、自治区房屋施工竣工面积

FLOOR SPACE OF BUILDINGS UNDER CONSTRUCTION AND COMPLETED BY REGION, 1995

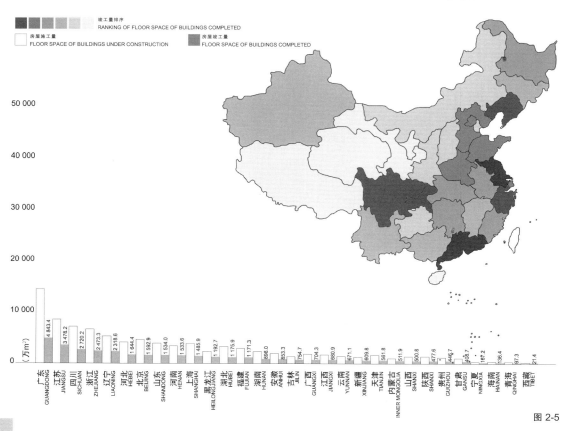

竣工量排序
RANKING OF FLOOR SPACE OF BUILDINGS COMPLETED

房屋施工量
FLOOR SPACE OF BUILDINGS UNDER CONSTRUCTION

房屋竣工量
FLOOR SPACE OF BUILDINGS COMPLETED

图 2-5

1995年，全国建设量增长较为迅速。从房屋建筑年度竣工面积上看，广东省以 4 843.4 万 m² 的房屋建筑竣工面积列在第一位。江苏、四川、浙江和辽宁分列第二至第五位，均超过了 2 000 万 m²。

国内各地区建设量之间的差别较大，1995 年广东省房屋建筑竣工面积约占全国的 14%。排名前五位的省份竣工面积之和占全国总竣工面积的 44%。

In 1995, the construction amount increased. From the perspective of annual building floor space completed, Guangdong took the 1st place with 48.434 million square meters. Jiangsu, Sichuan, Zhejiang and Liaoning took the 2nd to 5th place, all having exceeded 20 million square meters.

There is a great difference between regions, Guangdong's annual building floor spaces completed make up 14% of the national amount. Sum of the top five provinces accounted for 44% of the national total.

52

图 2-5 来源：陈瑾曼根据以下资料绘制,数据来源：中华人民共和国国家统计局，表 13-13 各地区房屋建筑面积:1996 中国统计年鉴. [EB/OL].1996 [2007-02-07].
http://www.stats.gov.cn/ndsj/information/zh1/m131a

2000年中国各省、市、自治区房屋施工竣工面积
FLOOR SPACE OF BUILDINGS UNDER CONSTRUCTION AND COMPLETED BY REGION, 2000

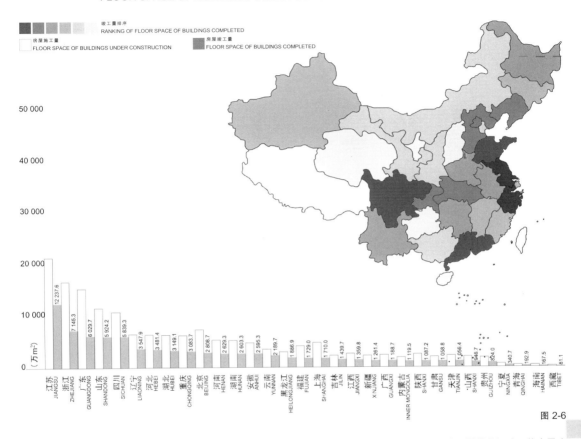

竣工量排序
RANKING OF FLOOR SPACE OF BUILDINGS COMPLETED

房屋施工量
FLOOR SPACE OF BUILDINGS UNDER CONSTRUCTION

房屋竣工量
FLOOR SPACE OF BUILDINGS COMPLETED

图 2-6

In 2000, the construction amount increased rapidly. From the standpoint of annual building floor space completed, Jiangsu took the 1st place with 122.376 million square meters, as well as being the only province having exceeded 100 million square meters. Zhejiang, Guangdong, Shandong and Sichuan ranked the 2nd to the 5th, all having exceeded 50 million square meters.

The difference between regions was widening. The Southeast and Sichuan in the midwestern China was leading. In 2000, Jiangsu's annual building floor space completed was 151 times that of Tibet, and accounted for 20% of the national amount. Sum of the top five provinces took up 46% of the national total, having increased 2 percent compared with that in 1995.

2000年，全国建设量增长迅速。从房屋建筑年度竣工面积上看,江苏省以 12 237.6 万 m² 的房屋建筑年度竣工面积列在首位，是惟一超过 10 000 万 m² 的省份。浙江、广东、山东和四川排在第二至第五位，房屋建筑年度竣工面积均超过了 5 000 万 m²。国内各地区建设量之间的差别拉大。东南沿海和中西部的四川省具有较多的建设量。2000 年江苏省房屋建筑竣工面积约占全国 20%，是西藏的 151 倍。排名前五的省份竣工面积之和占全国总竣工面积的 46%。比 1995 年增加了 2 个百分点。

图 2-6 来源：陈捷燕根据以下资料绘制。数据来源:中华人民共和国国家统计局，表 4-32 各地区房屋建筑面积地区房屋建筑面积:1996 中国统计年鉴。[EB/OL].1996
[2007-02-07].http://www.stats.gov.cn/tjsj/ndsj/2001c/n1432c.htm

2005年中国各省、市、自治区房屋施工竣工面积
FLOOR SPACE OF BUILDINGS UNDER CONSTRUCTION AND COMPLETED BY REGION, 2005

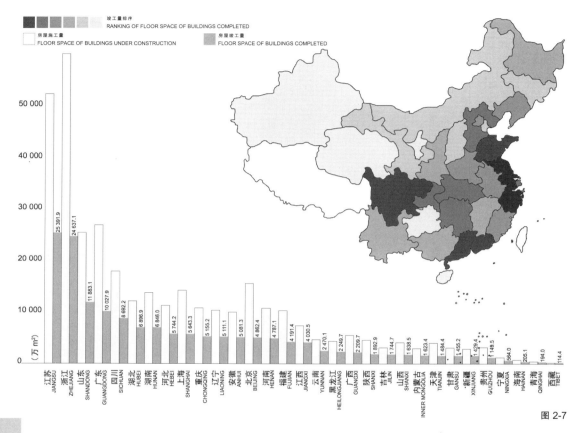

竣工量排序
RANKING OF FLOOR SPACE OF BUILDINGS COMPLETED

房屋施工量
FLOOR SPACE OF BUILDINGS UNDER CONSTRUCTION

房屋竣工量
FLOOR SPACE OF BUILDINGS COMPLETED

图 2-7

2005年，全国建设量增长更为迅速。从房屋建筑年度竣工面积上看，江苏以25 391.9万 m² 排在第一位。浙江、山东、广东和四川分列第二至第五位。其中江苏和浙江均超过了 20 000 万 m²，山东和广东超过了 10 000 万 m²。

国内各地区建设量之间的差别继续加大，东南沿海和中西部的四川具有较多的建设量。2005年江苏的房屋建筑竣工面积约占全国的 16%，而江苏和浙江两省则占全国的 31%。排名前五位省份竣工面积之和约占全国总竣工面积的 51%，比2000年上升了 5 个百分点。

In 2005, construction increased even more rapidly. From the standpoint of annual building floor space completed, Jiangsu still took the 1st place with 253.919 million square meters. Zhejiang, Shandong, Guangdong and Sichuan ranked the 2nd to the 5th, all having exceeded 100 million square meters.

The gap between regions continued widening. The Southeast and Sichuan continued to lead. In 2005, Jiangsu's annual completed building floor space accounted for 16% of the national amount, while the sum of Jiangsu and Zhejiang's made up 31%. Completed building floor space in the top five made up 51% of the national total, an increase of 5 percent compared to that in 2000.

图 2-7 来源：陈瑾羲根据以下资料绘制。数据来源：表 15-37 建筑业房屋建筑面积 [M]. // 中华人民共和国国家统计局 编. 2006 中国统计年鉴. 第一版. 北京：中国统计出版社, 2006:616

图 2-8

图 2-8 来源：陈瑾 根据以下资料改绘，图片来源：工地现场.
[EB/OL],2006,[2007-02-09].http://co.163.
cbm/forum/content/222_70665_1.htm

图 2-9 来源：陈瑾羲根据以下资料改绘 图片来源：土地进帖 [EB OL]
厦门房地产联合网. 2006 [2007-02-07].
http://bbs.xmhouse.com/scan/show_topic/?id=80859

图 2-9

2005年末中国各省、市、自治区城市实有建筑面积
TOTAL FLOOR SPACE OF URBAN BUILDINGS BY REGION, YEAR-END OF 2005

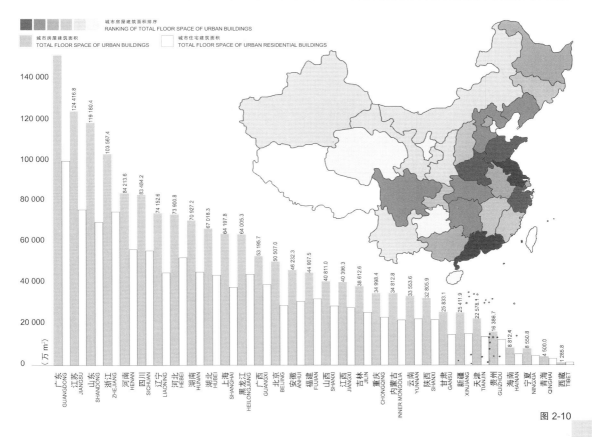

城市房屋建筑面积排序
RANKING OF TOTAL FLOOR SPACE OF URBAN BUILDINGS

城市房屋建筑面积
TOTAL FLOOR SPACE OF URBAN BUILDINGS

城市住宅建筑面积
TOTAL FLOOR SPACE OF URBAN RESIDENTIAL BUILDINGS

图 2-10

By the end of 2005, according to the actual urban building floor space by region, Guangdong took 1st place with 1 518.0797 million square meters. Jiangsu, Shandong, Zhejiang and Henan placed the 2nd to the 4th.

From the overall perspective of the whole country, a large gap existed between the regions. The eastern coastal area had the largest building floor spaces, the northeast and the central area had less, while the western region was placed at the bottom.

Besides, by the end of 2005, Guangdong still ranked the 1st according to real urban residential building floor space. Jiangsu, Zhejiang, Shandong and Henan rounded out the top five.

2005年末,广东省以 151 807.97 万 m² 排在首位。江苏、山东、浙江和河南分列第二至第四位。

从全国的分布来看,中国各省、市、自治区城市实有建筑面积差别较大。东部沿海地区拥有较多的城市实有建筑面积,东北地区和中部地区次之,西部地区较少。

2005 年末国内各省、市、自治区的城市住宅实有建筑面积仍以广东省位列首位,与江苏、浙江、山东和河南居于全国前五位。

图 2-10 来源: 陈瑾羲根据以下资料绘制.数据来源: 表 6-8 各地区全社会建设总规模[M].// 中华人民共和国国家统计局 编.2006 中国统计年鉴.第一版.北京: 中国统计出版社, 2006:616

57

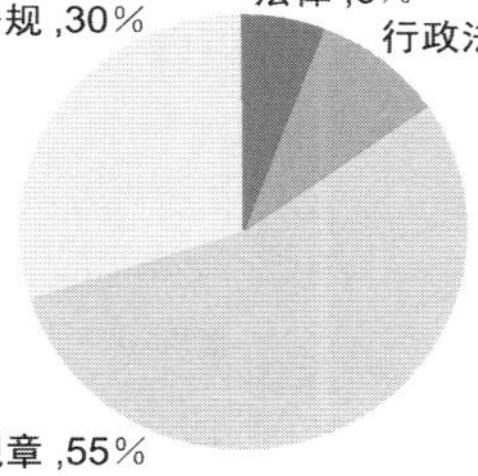

年份	法律	行政法规	部门规章	相关法规	全部法规
1980年	0	0	0	1	1
1981年	0	0	0	0	0
1982年	0	0	0	0	0
1983年	0	4	0	0	4
1984年	0	1	0	0	1
1985年	0	1	0	1	2
1986年	0	1	0	1	2
1987年	0	0	0	1	1
1988年	0	0	1	2	3
1989年	1	0	5	2	8
1990年	0	0	3	3	6
1991年	0	1	6	1	8
1992年	0	2	10	0	12
1993年	0	1	6	1	8
1994年	2	1	9	2	14
1995年	0	1	8	3	12
1996年	0	1	7	2	10
1997年	1	0	8	3	12
1998年	0	1	1	1	3
1999年	1	1	8	6	16
2000年	0	2	11	4	17
2001年	0	1	26	1	28
2002年	2	1	6	6	15
2003年	4	2	8	4	18
2004年	0	1	12	5	18
2005年	0	0	11	4	15
2006年	0	0	3	1	4
总数	11	23	149	55	238

图 2-11　现行建筑类各项法规所占比例

表 2-1　1980—2006 年中国颁布、修订和废止建设法规次数列表

现行建筑类法规共 181 部，具体包括：法律 11 部，占 6%；行政法规 17 部，占 9%；部门规章 98 部，占 55%；相关法规 55 部，占 30%。

There are 181 existing architectural laws and regulations, including 11 legal laws making up 6%, 17 administrative regulations at 9%, 98 departmental rules at 55%, as well as 55 relative regulations at 30% of the total.

表 2-1 来源：滕静茹根据以下资料绘制,数据来源：中华人民共和国建设部网站 [EB/OL],[2007-02-04].http://www.cin.gov.cn/law/main/
图 2-11 来源：滕静茹根据表 2-1 数据整理绘制

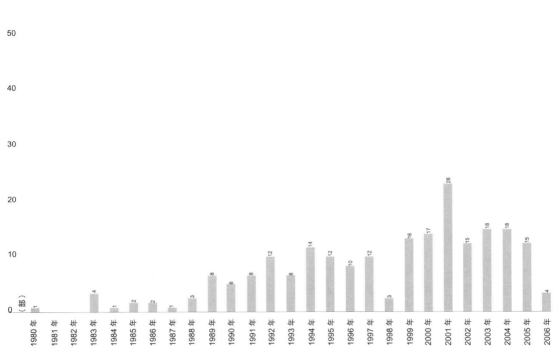

每年颁布、修订和废止建设法规次数
NUMBER OF CONSTRUCTION LAWS AND REGULATIONS PROMULGATED, AMENDED AND ABOLISHED YEARLY

图 2-12　1980—2006 年中国颁布、修订和废止建设法规次数

Since 1980, the Chinese government has promulgated a number of progressive legislations, to regulate the construction market and the construction industry. After 1990, the number of legislation increased.

1980年以来，中国政府逐步颁布了多项建筑法规以规范建筑行业和市场。1990 年以后，颁布的建筑法规数量呈增长趋势。

图 2-12 来源：滕静茹根据表 2-1 数据整理绘制

图片来源：陈瑞载改绘。资料来源：张耀 摄.奥运村工地塔吊最密集
[EB/OL].北京：北京日报,2006(2006-08-02)(2007-02-07).
http://epaper.bjd.com.cn/rb/20060802/200608/120060802_60226.htm

3 中国建筑设计机构

ARCHITECTURE DESIGN INFRASTRUCTURES OF CHINA

勘察设计企业(甲级)数量及分布
NUMBER AND DISTRIBUTION OF A-CLASS PROSPECTING AND DESIGNING INSTITUTIONS

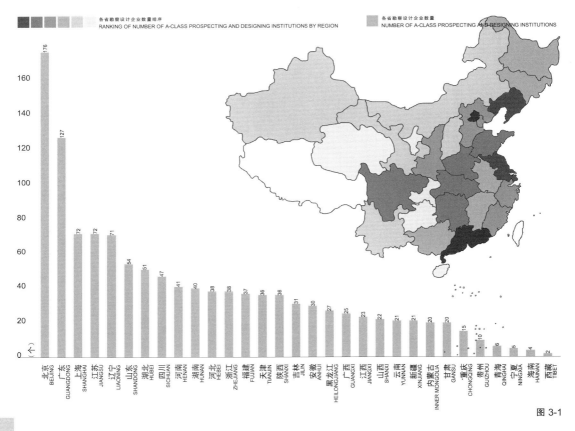

各省勘察设计企业数量排序
RANKING OF NUMBER OF A-CLASS PROSPECTING AND DESIGNING INSTITUTIONS BY REGION

各省勘察设计企业数量
NUMBER OF A-CLASS PROSPECTING AND DESIGNING INSTITUTIONS

图 3-1

根据中国房地产信息网公布数据整理，全国甲级的勘察设计企业共 1 218 家。从全国的分布情况看，北京以 176 家排在第一位，广东、上海、江苏和辽宁分列第二至第五位。第一、二位的北京和广东之间与并列第三位的上海和江苏在数量上差距较大。

根据建设部网站资料整理，2003 年中国勘察设计行业拥有甲级资质的占 16%，乙级占 28%，丙级占 34%，丁级占 5%，专项设计资质占 17%。

According to data collated by the website of www.realestate.gov.cn , analysis revealed that there are 1 218 A-class prospecting and designing institutions all through the country. According to the national distribution, Beijing placed the 1st place with 176, along with Guangdong, Shanghai, Jiangsu and Liaoning took the top five places. The 1st and 2nd region, Beijing and Guangdong led by a large advantage over the 3rd place tie between Shanghai and Jiangsu. According to data collated from the Ministry of Construction of China website , in 2003, A-class prospecting and design institutions accounted for 16% of the class endowment, B-class accounted for 28%, C-class accounted for 34%, D-class accounted for 5%, while special design quality accounted for 17%.

图 3-1 来源：陈璀蓉根据以下资料绘制,数据来源：中国房地产信息网（中华人民共和国建设部住宅与房地产业司主办，建设部信息中心、建设部新闻宣传中心承办）,甲级勘察设计企业[EB/OL]，北京 [2007-02-04].http://www.realestate.gov.cn/qualif-ication.asp?teamno=145&line=5&outwhereclause=%20(%20Cclassid=21)&secsortno=grade
图 3-2 来源：腾静茹根据以下资料改绘,图片来源：中华人民共和国建设部网站（中华人民共和国建设部主办，建设部信息中心承办）,勘察设计行业 2003 年资质等级分布图示[EB/OL].[2007-02-04].http://www.cin.gov.cn/quality/statis/ts_02.htm

丁级,5%   专项,17%
丙级,34%   甲级,16%
乙级,28%   乙级,28%
图 3-2

城市规划编制单位(甲级)数量及分布
NUMBER AN DISTRIBUTION OF A-CLASS URBAN PLANNING INSTITUTIONS

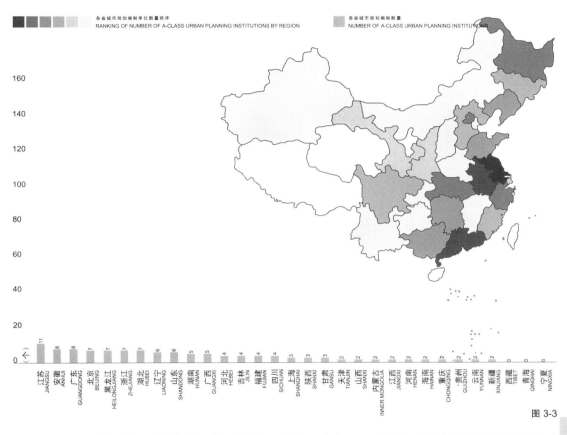

各省城市规划编制单位数量排序
RANKING OF NUMBER OF A-CLASS URBAN PLANNING INSTITUTIONS BY REGION

各省城市规划编制数量
NUMBER OF A-CLASS URBAN PLANNING INSTITUTIONS

图 3-3

According to data collated from the Ministry of Construction of China website, analysis revealed that the number of China's current A-Class urban planning institutions is 122.

In terms of national distribution, Jiangsu, with 11 institutions took the 1st place, Anhui and Guangdong tied for the second with 8 each, while Beijing, Heilongjiang, Zhejiang and Hubei had 7 each, for a tie at fourth. Tibet, Qinghai and Ningxia had no A-Class credential urban planning institutions currently.

根据中华人民共和国建设部网站公布的数据整理，中国现有甲级资质城市规划编制单位共 122 家。

从全国的分布来看，江苏以 11 家列在首位，安徽、广东各有 8 家并列第二位，北京、黑龙江、浙江和湖北有 7 家，并列第四位。而西藏、青海和宁夏尚没有甲级资质城市规划编制单位。

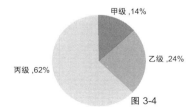

甲级 ,14%

乙级 ,24%

丙级 ,62%

图 3-4

图 3-3 来源：陈瑾羲根据以下资料绘制.数据来源：中华人民共和国建设部网站
(中华人民共和国建设部主办，建设部信息中心承办)，资质管理
[EB/OL],[2007-02-04].http://www.cin.gov.cn/Planning/zz/ 资质管理
图 3-4 来源：根据以下资料绘制.数据来源：中国城市规划协会网站（中国城市规划协会主办）甲级资质单位名称、乙级资质单位名称、丙级资质单位名称
[EB/OL],[2007-02-04].
http://www.cacp.org.cn/level/level.asp?level= 甲级、
http://www.cacp.org.cn/level/level.asp?level= 乙级、
http://www.cacp.org.cn/level/level.asp?level= 丙级.

一级注册建筑师数量及分布
NUMBER AND DISTRIBUTION OF A-CLASS REGISTERD ARCHITECTS

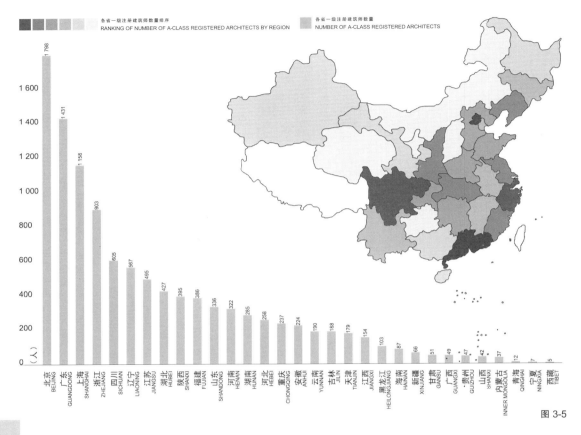

图 3-5

根据中华人民共和国建设部网站公布数据统计，至2007年1月，全国一级注册建筑师的数量共11 044人。

从全国的分布情况看，北京以1 798人排在第一位，约占全国的16％。广东、上海、浙江和四川分列第二至第五位，均超过了600人。排名前五位的省份一级注册建筑师数量之和约占全国的53％。

According to statistics from the website of the Ministry of Construction of China, up to Jan. 2007, China had a total of 11 044 registered A-class architects.

From the national distribution data, Beijing was ranked the 1st with 1 798, accounting for 16% of the national total. Guangdong, Shanghai, Zhejiang and Sichuan placed the 2nd to the 5th place, all exceeding 600 people. The top five accounted for about 53% of the national total.

图 3-5 来源：陈瑾羲根据以下资料绘制,数据来源：中华人民共和国建设部网站
(中华人民共和国建设部主办，建设部信息中心承办) .全国一级注册建筑师查询
[EB/OL],2007(2007-01-26)[2007-02-04].
http://www.cin.gov.cn/register/jzs/default.htm.

注册规划师数量及分布
NUMBER AND DISTRIBUTION OF REGISTERD URBAN PLANNERS

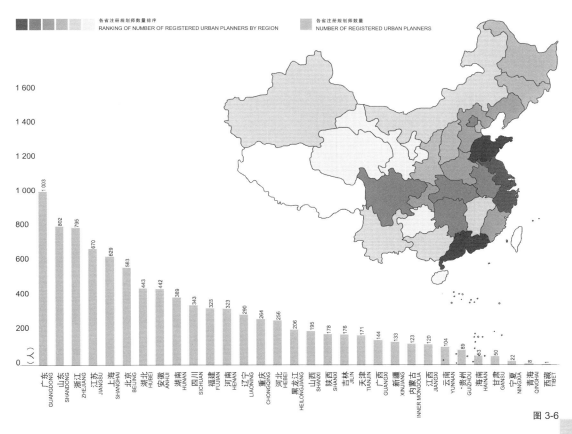

各省注册规划师数量排序
RANKING OF NUMBER OF REGISTERED URBAN PLANNERS BY REGION

各省注册规划师数量
NUMBER OF REGISTERED URBAN PLANNERS

图 3-6

According to data from the Ministry of Construction of China website, statistics revealed that, by the end of 2006, there were 9 313 registered urban planners in China.

From the national distribution, Guangdong took the 1st place with 1 003 people, accounting for 10% of the national total. Shandong, Zhejiang, Jiangsu and Shanghai placed the 2nd to the 5th place, all exceeding 600 people. The Top 5 regions accounted for about 42% of the national total.

根据中华人民共和国建设部网站公布数据统计，至 2006 年底，全国注册规划师的数量共 9 313 人。

从全国的分布情况看，广东以 1 003 人排在第一位，占全国注册规划师人数的 10%，远远领先于其他省份。山东、浙江、江苏和上海分列第二至第五位，均超过了 600 人。排名前五位的省份注册规划师数量之和约占全国的 42%。

图 3-6 来源：滕静茹根据以下资料绘制.数据来源：中华人民共和国建设部网站 (中华人民共和国建设部主办，建设部信息中心承办).注册城市规划师初始注册登记人员名单，[EB/OL].[2007-02-04]
http://www.cin.gov.cn/indus/notice/2006031403.htm; http://www.cin.gov.cn/Planning/file/2006060903.htm; http://www.cin.gov.cn/Planning/file/2006090701.htm; http://www.cin.gov.cn/indus/notice/2006110202.htm.

各省、市、自治区每百万人一级注册建筑师数量

NUMBER OF A-CLASS REGISTERED ARCHITECTS PER MILLION PEOPLE BY REGION

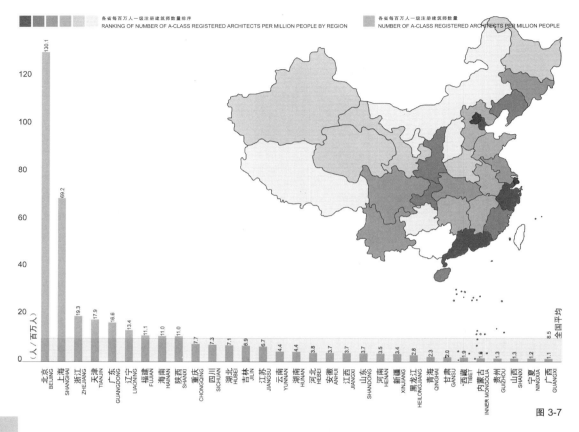

各省每百万人一级注册建筑师数量排序
RANKING OF NUMBER OF A-CLASS REGISTERED ARCHITECTS PER MILLION PEOPLE BY REGION

各省每百万人一级注册建筑师数量
NUMBER OF A-CLASS REGISTERED ARCHITECTS PER MILLION PEOPLE

130.1 北京 BEIJING
69.2 上海 SHANGHAI
19.3 浙江 ZHEJIANG
17.9 天津 TIANJIN
16.6 广东 GUANGDONG
13.4 辽宁 LIAONING
11.1 福建 FUJIAN
11.0 海南 HAINAN
11.0 陕西 SHANXI
7.7 重庆 CHONGQING
7.3 四川 SICHUAN
7.1 湖北 HUBEI
6.9 吉林 JILIN
6.7 江苏 JIANGSU
4.4 云南 YUNNAN
4.4 湖南 HUNAN
3.8 河北 HEBEI
3.7 安徽 ANHUI
3.7 江西 JIANGXI
3.7 山东 SHANDONG
3.5 河南 HENAN
3.4 新疆 XINJIANG
2.8 黑龙江 HEILONGJIANG
2.3 青海 QINGHAI
2.0 甘肃 GANSU
1.9 西藏 TIBET
1.6 内蒙古 INNER MONGOLIA
1.3 贵州 GUIZHOU
1.3 山西 SHANXI
1.2 宁夏 NINGXIA
1.1 广西 GUANGXI

8.5 全国平均

(人／百万人)

图 3-7

根据中华人民共和国建设部网站公布的数据以及第五次人口普查数据统计，截至2007年1月26号，中国全国每百万人一级注册建筑师数量为8.5人。超过全国平均水平的地区共有9个。

从全国的分布来看，北京以130.1人/百万人列在第一位，上海以69.2人/百万人列在第二位，浙江、天津和广东分列前三至第五位。

全国各省市自治区差距较大，北京、上海与其他省份相比具有很大的优势。北京每百万人均建筑师数量是上海的近2倍，是广西的118倍，约为全国平均数的15倍。

According to data released on the Ministry of Construction of China website and the fifth census, by Jan. 26, 2007, the number of registered A-class architects per million was about 8.5. There were 9 provinces exceeding the national average level.

Analyzing the national distribution, Beijing took the 1st place with 130.1 registered A-class architects per million people; Shanghai took the 2nd place with the number of 69.2 per million. Zhejiang, Tianjin and Guangdong took the 3rd to the 5th place.

A big gap existed between the country's various provinces, cities and autonomous regions: Beijing and Shanghai led by a tremendous advantage over other regions. Beijing's was nearly 2 times that of Shanghai, and 118 times that of Guangxi, about 15 times the national average.

图 3-7 来源：陈瑾羲根据以下资料绘制. 中华人民共和国建设部网站（中华人民共和国建设部主办，建设部信息中心承办）. 全国一级注册建筑师查询 [EB/OL] [2007-01-24].
http://www.cin.gov.cn/registre/jzs/default.htm；中华人民共和国国家统计局网站（中华人民共和国国家统计局主办），第五次全国人口普查公报[EB/OL]. [2007-01-26].
http://www.stats.gov.cn/was40/gjtjj_detail.jsp?channelid=2912&record=41.20061224

各省、市、自治区每百万人注册规划师数量
NUMBER OF REGISTERED URBAN PLANNERS PER MILLION PEOPLE BY REGION

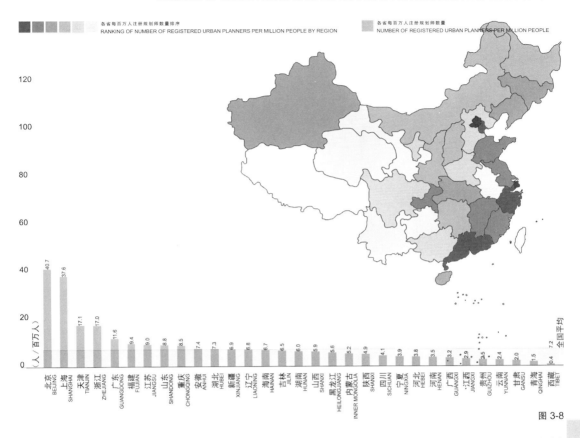

图 3-8

According to data released on the Ministry of Construction of China website and the fifth census, analysis revealed that in 2006, the number of registered urban planners per million was about 7.2. There were 11 provinces exceeding the national average level.

Analyzing the national distribution, Beijing took the 1st place with 40.7 urban planners per million people. Shanghai took the 2nd place with 37.6 per million. Tianjin, Zhejiang, and Guangdong placed the 3rd to the 5th place.

A big gap existed between the country's various provinces, cities and autonomous regions: Beijing and Shanghai led a tremendous advantage over the other regions. Beijing's is almost 101 times that of Tibet, and about 6 times the national average.

根据中华人民共和国建设部网站公布的数据以及第五次人口普查数据整理，2006 年全国每百万人注册规划师数量为 7.2 人。超过全国平均水平的地区共有 11 个。

从全国各省的分布来看，北京以 40.7 人／百万人排在第一位，上海以 37.6 人／百万人排在第二位，天津、浙江和广东分列第三至第五位。

全国各省市自治区的差距很大，北京、上海与其他地区相比具有明显优势。北京每百万人注册规划师数量是西藏的 101 倍，约是全国平均数的近 6 倍。

图 3-8 来源：陈璐莪根据以下资料绘制. 数据来源：中华人民共和国建设部网站 （中华人民共和国建设部主办，建设部信息中心承办）. 注册城市规划师初始注册登记人员名单 [EB/OL].[2007-02-04]
http://www.cin.gov.cn/indus/notice/2006031403.htm ;
http://www.cin.gov.cn/Planning/file/2006060903.htm ;
http://www.cin.gov.cn/Planning/file/2006090701.htm ;
http://www.cin.gov.cn/indus/notice/2006110202.htm;
中华人民共和国国家统计局网站 （中华人民共和国国家统计局主办）. 第五次全国人口普查公报 [EB/OL].[2007-02-04].http://www.stats.gov.cn/was40/gjtjj_detail.jsp?channelid=2912&record=41.20061224.

中国科学院建筑、规划、风景园林专业院士名录
MEMBER OF CHINESE ACADEMY OF SCIENCE,
MAJOR OF ARCHITECTURE, URBAN PLANNING AND LANDSCAPE ARCHITECTURE

注：按照当选为中国科学院院士时间排序，当选时间相同的按照出生时间排序

姓名	当选为中国科学院院士时间	出生时间
梁思成	1955年	1901年
杨廷宝	1955年	1901年
刘敦桢	1955年	1897年
吴良镛	1980年	1922年
周干峙	1991年	1930年
戴念慈	1991年	1920年
齐康	1993年	1931年
彭一刚	1995年	1932年
郑时龄	2001年	1941年
吴硕贤	2005年	1947年

表 3-1

梁思成

杨廷宝

刘敦桢

吴良镛

周干峙

戴念慈

齐 康

彭一刚

郑时龄

吴硕贤

图 3-9

据中国科学院学部与院士网和中国工程院网页公布数据统计，截至 2007 年 2 月，建筑、规划、风景园林专业的院士总席位为 25 个，院士人数为 23 人。其中吴良镛和周干峙为两院院士。院士总人数占全国一级注册建筑师和注册规划师数量的 0.11％。

建筑和城市规划专业的中国科学院院士共 10 人，占技术科学部院士总数的 4.4％，占中国科学院院士总数的 0.8％。其中梁思成、杨廷宝、刘敦桢和戴念慈已经去世。

表 3-1 来源：陈瑾羲根据以下资料绘制,数据来源：中国科学院学部与院士网.
技术科学部院士介绍, [EB/OL].北京：中国科学院院士工作局，
2007[2007-02-07].http://www.casad.ac.cn/viewdept.asp?id=6
图 3-9 来源：陈瑾羲根据以下资料改绘.照片来源：人民网.技术科学部院士名
单.[EB/OL].北京：人民网, 2003(2003-09-25)[2007-02-07].
http://www.people.com.cn/mediafile/200309/25/F2003092509551500000.jpg;
http://www.people.com.cn/GB/keji/25509/29829/2108932.html;
http://www.people.com.cn/GB/keji/25509/29829/2108540.html;
http://www.people.com.cn/GB/keji/25509/29829/2108861.html;
http://www.people.com.cn/GB/keji/25509/29829/2109061.html;
http://www.people.com.cn/GB/keji/25509/29829/2108352.html;
http://www.people.com.cn/GB/keji/25509/29829/2108605.html;
http://www.people.com.cn/GB/keji/25509/29829/2108602.html;
http://www.people.com.cn/GB/keji/25509/29829/2109027.html;
http://www.gdzs114.com/edu/UploadFiles_8366/200606/20060628093329680.jpg

According to data released on the Division of the Chinese Academy of Sciences and Chinese Academy of Engineering website, statistics revealed that by Feb. 2007, architecture, urban planning and landscape architecture professional academicians took a total of 25 seats, with 23 academicians, of which Mr. Wu Liangyong and Mr.Zhou Ganzhi belong to both academies. The total number from both academies accounted for 0.11% of the number of national registered A-class architects and urban planners.

The number of architecture and urban planning professionals in the Chinese Academy of Sciences is 10, accounting for 4.4% of the department of science and technology, and making up 0.8% of the total number of academicians of the Chinese Academy of Sciences. From the list, Liang Sicheng, Yang Tingbao, Liu Dunzhen and Dai Nianci have passed away.

中国工程院建筑、规划、风景园林专业院士名录
MEMBER OF CHINESE ACADEMY OF ENGINEERING,
MAJOR OF ARCHITECTURE, URBAN PLANNING AND LANDSCAPE ARCHITECTURE

注：按照当选为中国工程院院士时间排序，当选时间相同的按照出生时间排序

 周干峙   傅熹年   张锦秋   吴良镛

 关肇邺   钟训正   马国馨   戴复东

李道增   孟兆祯   何镜堂   魏敦山

邹德慈   王瑞珠   程泰宁

姓名	当选为中国工程院院士时间	出生时间
周干峙	1994年	1930年
傅熹年	1994年	1933年
张锦秋	1994年	1936年
吴良镛	1995年	1922年
关肇邺	1995年	1929年
钟训正	1997年	1929年
马国馨	1997年	1942年
戴复东	1999年	1928年
李道增	1999年	1930年
孟兆祯	1999年	1932年
何镜堂	1999年	1938年
魏敦山	2001年	1933年
邹德慈	2003年	1934年
王瑞珠	2003年	1940年
程泰宁	2005年	1935年

表 3-2

图 3-10

According to data released on the Division of the Chinese Academy of Engineering website, statistics revealed that by Feb. 2007, there were 698 academicians in the Chinese Academy of Engineering. Architecture, urban planning and landscape architecture professional academicians took 15 seats, accounting for 17% of department of civil and construction engineering, and accounting for 2.3% of the total number of academicians of the Chinese Academy of Engineering.

据中国工程院网页公布数据统计，截至2007年2月，中国工程院院士人数共698人。建筑、规划、风景园林专业的中国工程院院士共15人，占土木、水利与建筑工程学部院士数量的17%，占所有中国工程院院士总数的2.3%。

表 3-2 来源：陈瑾羲根据以下资料绘制.数据来源：中国工程院院士信息 - 土木、水利与建筑工程学部，[EB/OL].北京：中国工程院，2006[2007-02-07].http://www.cae.cn/experts/index.jsp?subCid1=tm
图 3-10 来源：陈瑾羲根据以下资料改绘.照片来源：中国工程院院士信息 - 土木、水利与建筑工程学部，[EB/OL].北京：中国工程院，2006[2007-02-07].
http://www.cae.cn/admin/upload/img/maguoxin.jpg;
http://www.cae.cn/admin/upload/img/wangruizhu.jpg;
http://www.cae.cn/admin/upload/img/guanzhaoye.jpg;
http://www.cae.cn/admin/upload/img/jiangyi.jpg;
http://www.cae.cn/admin/upload/img/hejingtang.jpg;
http://www.cae.cn/admin/upload/img/wuliangyong.jpg;
http://www.cae.cn/admin/upload/img/zhangjinqiu.jpg;
http://www.cae.cn/admin/upload/img/lidaozeng.jpg;
http://www.cae.cn/admin/upload/img/zoudeci.jpg;
http://www.cae.cn/admin/upload/img/zhouganchi.jpg;
http://www.cae.cn/admin/upload/img/mengzhaozhen.jpg;
http://www.cae.cn/admin/upload/img/zhongxunzheng.jpg;
http://www.cae.cn/admin/upload/img/fuxinan.jpg;
http://www.cae.cn/admin/upload/img/chengtaining.jpg;
http://www.cae.cn/admin/upload/img/daifudong.jpg;
http://www.cae.cn/admin/upload/img/weidunshan.jpg

中国建筑设计大师名录
ARCHITECTURE DESIGN MASTERS

获奖批次	获奖时间	姓名
第一批	1990年	齐 康
第一批	1990年	孙国城
第一批	1990年	严星华
第一批	1990年	佘竣南
第一批	1990年	陈 植
第一批	1990年	陈浩荣
第一批	1990年	陈登鳌
第一批	1990年	张 镈
第一批	1990年	张开济
第一批	1990年	张锦秋
第一批	1990年	赵冬日
第一批	1990年	徐尚志
第一批	1990年	龚德顺
第一批	1990年	熊 明
第一批	1990年	戴念慈

获奖批次	获奖时间	姓名
第三批	2000年	何玉如
第三批	2000年	程泰宁
第三批	2000年	关肇邺
第三批	2000年	胡绍学
第三批	2000年	彭一刚
第三批	2000年	崔 恺
第三批	2000年	赵冠谦
第三批	2000年	黄星元
第三批	2000年	刘景樑
第三批	2000年	李高岚
第三批	2000年	黎佗芬
第三批	2000年	黄锡璆

获奖批次	获奖时间	姓名
第二批	1994年	马国馨
第二批	1994年	刘纯翰
第二批	1994年	刘克良
第二批	1994年	何镜堂
第二批	1994年	陈世民
第二批	1994年	周方中
第二批	1994年	饶维纯
第二批	1994年	袁培煌
第二批	1994年	徐庆延
第二批	1994年	莫伯治
第二批	1994年	郭怡昌
第二批	1994年	黄克武
第二批	1994年	蔡镇钰
第二批	1994年	魏敦山

获奖批次	获奖时间	姓名
第四批	2004年	刘 力
第四批	2004年	柴斐义
第四批	2004年	郭明卓
第四批	2004年	沈济黄
第四批	2004年	吴庐生
第四批	2004年	张家臣
第四批	2004年	唐葆亨
第四批	2004年	郑国英
第四批	2004年	时 匡
第四批	2004年	唐玉恩

获奖批次	获奖时间	姓名
第五批	2006年	孟建民
第五批	2006年	胡 越

表 3-3

70

截止到 2006 年底，勘察设计大师中建筑设计专业共 53 人，占勘察设计大师总数 14%，占一级注册建筑师总数 4.9%。

By the end of 2006, there were 53 professional architecture design masters, accounting for 14% of the total Exploration and Design Masters, making up 4.9% of the total number of A-class registered architects.

表 3-3 来源：腾静茹绘制；资料来源：
中国勘察设计协会.第一批勘察设计大师 120 人(1990 年) [EB/OL].北京：中国勘察设计协会，2005[2007-01-20].
http://www.chinaeda.org/artDetail.asp?id=662;
中国勘察设计协会.1994 年颁布的第二批勘察设计大师 [EB/OL].北京：中国勘察设计协会，2005[2007-01-20].
http://www.chinaeda.org/artDetail.asp?id=660;
中国勘察设计协会.全国工程勘察设计大师（第三批）名单 [EB/OL].北京：中国勘察设计协会，2005[2007-01-20].
http://www.chinaeda.org/artDetail.asp?id=663;
中华人民共和国建设部.中华人民共和国建设部公告第 234 号;关于公布全国第四批勘察设计大师名单的公告 [EB/OL].北京：中华人民共和国建设部，2004[2006-09-18].
http://www.cin.gov.cn/indus/notice/2004051301.htm;
中华人民共和国建设部.中华人民共和国建设部公告第 534 号;关于第五批全国工程勘察设计大师名单的公告 [EB/OL].北京：中华人民共和国建设部，2004[2007-01-20]. http://www.cin.gov.cn/quality/tech/2006123005.htm.

建筑设计大师占勘察设计大师比例

PROPORTION OF ARCHITECTURE DESIGN MASTERS AMONG THE EXPLORATION AND DESIGN MASTERS

建筑设计,14%
其他专业,86%

建筑设计大师占总勘察设计
大师的比例

建筑设计,13%
其他专业,87%

第一批建筑设计大师占第一
批总勘察设计大师的比例

建筑设计,12%
其他专业,88%

第二批建筑设计大师占第二
批总勘察设计大师的比例

建筑设计,20%
其他专业,80%

第三批建筑设计大师占第三
批勘察设计大师的比例

建筑设计,17%
其他专业,83%

第四批建筑设计大师占第四
批总勘察设计大师的比例

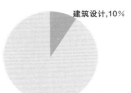

建筑设计,10%
其他专业,90%

第五批建筑设计大师占第五
批总勘察设计大师的比例

图 3-11

In 1990, the first batch of Exploration and Design Masters had 120 people, of which 15 were architectural design professionals. The second batch of Exploration and Design Masters contained 121 people in 1994, with 14 architectural design professionals. The third batch included 60 people in 2000, with 12 architectural design professionals. The fourth batch was awarded to 60 people in 2004, with 10 architectural design professionals. While the fifth batch was awarded to 21 people in 2006, including 2 architectural design professionals.

1990年评选出第一批全国勘察设计大师共120人,其中建筑设计专业15人。
1994 年评选出第二批全国勘察设计大师共 121 人,其中建筑设计专业 14 人。
2000 年评选出第三批全国勘察设计大师共 60 人,其中建筑设计专业 12 人。
2004 年评选出第四批全国勘察设计大师共 60 人,其中建筑设计专业 10 人。
2006 年评选出第五批全国勘察设计大师共 21 人,其中建筑设计专业 2 人。

图 3-11 来源:陈瑾羲根据表 3-3 资料整理绘制

4 中国建筑媒体

ARCHITECTURE MEDIA OF CHINA

建筑期刊博览
A BRIEF REVIEW OF ARCHITECTURE JOURNALS

一、建筑学期刊

刊名：建筑学报
Architectural Journal
主办：中国建筑学会
出版地：北京市
创刊年：1954

刊名：世界建筑
World Architecture
主办：清华大学建筑学院
出版地：北京市
创刊年：1980

刊名：建筑师
Architect
主办：中国建筑工业出版社
出版地：北京市
创刊年：2003

刊名：时代建筑
Time + Architecture
主办：同济大学建筑与城市
规划学院
出版地：上海市
创刊年：1984

刊名：新建筑
New Architecture
主办：华中科技大学
出版地：武汉市
创刊年：1983

刊名：华中建筑
Huazhong Architecture
主办：中南建筑设计院；湖北土
木建筑学会
出版地：武汉市
创刊年：1983

刊名：建筑创作
Architectural Creation
主办：北京市建筑设计研究院
出版地：北京市
创刊年：1989

刊名：世界建筑导报
World Architecture Review
主办：深圳大学
出版地：深圳市
创刊年：1985

二、城市规划期刊

刊名：建筑史
Architecture History
主办：清华大学建筑学院
出版地：北京市
创刊年：1964

刊名：城市建筑
Urbanism and Architecture
主办：哈尔滨工业大学建筑学
院
出版地：哈尔滨市
创刊年：2004

刊名：城市环境设计
Urban Space Design
主办：天津大学建筑学院
出版地：沈阳市
创刊年：2004

刊名：城市规划
City Planning Review
主办：中国城市规划学会
出版地：北京市
创刊年：1977

刊名：国外城市规划
Urban Planning Overseas
主办：中国城市规划设计研究院
出版地：北京市
创刊年：1979

刊名：城市规划学刊
Urban Planning Forum
主办：同济大学建筑与城市规
划学院
出版地：上海市
创刊年：1957

刊名：规划师
Planners
主办：广西建筑综合设计研究院
出版地：南宁市
创刊年：1985

刊名：小城镇建设
Development of Small Cities &
Towns
主办：中国建筑设计研究院
出版地：北京市
创刊年：1983

74

作为建筑领域的媒介之一，建筑期刊一直扮演着重要的角色。1980 年以来，建筑期刊进入了大发展时期。

以 32 种建筑领域主要期刊为例，从数量上看，90％的刊物创办于 1978 年以后。从创办主体上看，从 1978 年前单纯的中央机构主办，发展到今天的以建筑院校、设计院、公司为期刊主办的生力军。

同时，90 年代出现的住宅类期刊以及 2000 年以来国外期刊中国版的兴起也成为了建筑期刊业新的时代特点。

As one of the media in architecture fields, architecture Journals have played important roles. Since 1980, architecture Journals have entered a period of great development.

Taking 32 kinds of architecture Journals as an example, 90% of those were founded after 1978 . It can be found that types of sponsors developed from the pure governmental organization before 1978 to architecture schools, design institutes, companies nowadays.

Meanwhile, the housing Journals appeared in the 1990s as well as the China version of overseas Journals have appeared since 2000. Those Journals also become new characteristic of the architecture Journals.

图 4-1 秦臻根据以下绘制 图片来源：中国知网.[EB/OL]，http://ckrd.cnki.net
图 4-2 秦臻统计绘制
图 4-3 秦臻统计绘制
图 4-4 秦臻统计绘制

三、风景园林、室内设计及其他

刊名：北京规划建设
Beijing Planning Review
主办：北京城市规划设计研究院
出版地：北京市
创刊年：1987

刊名：上海城市规划
Shanghai Urban Planning Review
主办：上海市城市规划管理局
出版地：上海市
创刊年：1995

刊名：风景园林
Landscape Arehitecture
主办：北京林业大学
出版地：深圳市
创刊年：1993

刊名：中国园林
Journal of Chinese Landscape Architecture
主办：中国风景园林学会
出版地：北京市
创刊年：1985

刊名：装饰
Art & Design
主办：清华大学美术学院
出版地：北京市
创刊年：1958

刊名：室内设计与装修
Interior Design Construction
主办：南京林业大学
出版地：南京市
创刊年：1986

刊名：室内设计
Interior Design
主办：重庆大学
出版地：重庆市
创刊年：1986

刊名：建筑技术及设计
Architecture Technology & Design
主办：中国建筑技术研究院
出版地：北京市
创刊年：1994

四、国外引进杂志

刊名：住区
Design Community
主办：清华大学建筑设计研究院
出版地：北京市
创刊年：2004

刊名：城市住宅
City Residence
主办：中国建筑设计研究院
出版地：北京市
创刊年：1994

刊名：建筑实录
Architectural Record
主办：中国建筑工业出版社
出版地：北京市
创刊年：2004
原版地：美国

刊名：Domus 国际中国版
主办：Sinius International
出版地：北京市
创刊年：2006
原版地：意大利

刊名：ELCroquis
主办：宁波出版社
出版地：宁波市
创刊年：2005
原版地：西班牙

刊名：Landscape Design
主办：MARUMO Publishing Co., Ltd,Japan
出版地：大连市
创刊年：2004
原版地：日本

刊名：a+u
主办：宁波出版社
周期：双月刊
出版地：宁波市
创刊年：2004
原版地：日本

刊名：建筑细部
Architecture & Detail
主办：大连理工大学
出版地：大连市
创刊年：2003
原版地：德国

图 4-1

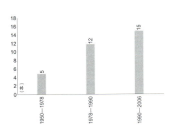

图 4-2　32 本建筑期刊创刊年代

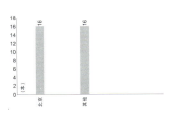

图 4-3　32 本建筑期刊地理分布

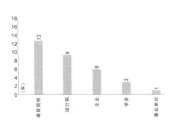

图 4-4　32 本建筑期刊主办主体

建筑网站导航
A BRIEF REVIEW OF ARCHITECTUARAL WEBSITES

政府部门、学会网站
WEBSITES OF GOVERNMENTS & ASSOCIATIONS

中国建设部网站由中华人民共和国建设部主办，是建设部发布信息的官方权威网站。
http://www.cin.gov.cn/

中国工程建设信息网是建设部主办，该网站向社会发布工程信息、政策法规信息、企业状况信息等。
http://www.cein.gov.cn/

中国建筑学会网站由中国建筑学会主办，主要针对中国建筑学会会员服务。
http://www.chinaasc.org/

中国城市规划学会网站
http://www.planning.org.cn/

北京市规划委员会的官方网站，是有关首都规划建设信息的发布平台。
http://www.bjghw.gov.cn/

上海市规划局的官方网站，是有关上海规划建设信息的发布平台。
http://www.shghj.gov.cn/

设计院网站
WEBSITES OF ARCHITECTURE DESIGN INSTITUTES

中国建筑设计研究院网站
http://www.cadreg.com.cn/

中国城市规划设计研究院网站
http://www.caupd.com/

北京市建筑设计研究院网站
http://www.shghj.gov.cn/

上海现代建筑设计（集团）有限公司网站
http://www.xd-ad.com.cn/

清华大学建筑设计研究院网站
http://www.thad.com.cn/

同济大学建筑设计研究院网站
http://www.tjadri.com/

建筑网站已经成为了建筑领域不可或缺的沟通工具和信息窗口，建筑网站使得建筑师之间足不出户便可以实现资源的共享。建筑网站门类众多，大致可以分为以下几种类型：政府部门、学会网站；设计研究院、事务所、设计咨询公司网站；各建筑院校网站；非政府建筑网站及博客等。

Architectural websites have become indispensable communication tools and windows to get information for architects. Architects can share their resources indoors. Nowadays, architectural websites have many types, including websites of government and the associations; websites of design institutes, firms, companies; websites of architectural schools; the non-governmental architectural websites; blog, etc.

清华大学建筑学院网站
http://www.arch.tsinghua.edu.cn/

天津大学建筑学院网站
http://202.113.13.67/colleges/architecture/

西安建筑科技大学建筑学院网站
http://www.xauat.edu.cn/yxsz/jianzhu/

东南大学建筑学院网站
http://arch.seu.edu.cn/

重庆大学建筑城规学院网站
http://www.chongjian.com/

华南理工大学建筑学院网站
http://www2.scut.edu.cn/

同济大学建筑城规学院网站
http://www.tongji-caup.org/

哈尔滨工业大学建筑学院网站
http://jzxy.hit.edu.cn/index/

非政府建筑网站
NON—GOVERNMENTAL ARCHITECTURAL WEBSITES

ABBS 网站成立于 1998 年 6 月 18 日， 以论坛形式为主。
是建筑领域知名的网站。
http://www.abbs.com.cn/

FAR2000 网站是北京水晶石电脑图像公司投资的建筑网
站， 提供国内外建筑师检索， 设计招标发布、 设计方案
及资源。
http://www.far2000.com/

筑龙网创建于 1998 年底， 是建筑行业电子技术资料下载
平台和信息交流平台， 是行业内第一个收费网站。
http://www.sinoaec.com/

建筑英才网成立于 2001 年 4 月， 是专业为建筑设计、 房
地产、 工程类企、 事业单位以及相关从业人员提供招聘、
求职、 人才测评、 培训等服务的人才网站。
http://www.buildhr.com/

由于竞赛种类繁多，"中国建筑竞赛"一章仅汇总了从 1978 年至 2006 年《建筑学报》刊登的设计竞赛。

Because of the great number of competitions, the chapter "Architecture Competitions of China" only collects architecture compettions published in *Architecture Journal* from 1978 to 2006.

图片来源：陈瑾羲改绘。资料来源：张耀 摄.奥运村工地塔吊墨迹集 [EB/OL].
北京：北京日报,2006(2006-08-02)[2007-02-07].
http://epaper.bjd.com.cn/rb/20060802/200808/20060802_60226.htm

5 中国建筑竞赛
ARCHITECTURE COMPETITIONS OF CHINA

建筑竞赛——以《建筑学报》（1978－2006）为例

A COLLECTION OF ARCHITECTURAL COMPETITIONS BASED ON ARCHITECTURAL JOURNAL(1978-2006)

竞赛名称	举办者	参赛作品	举办地	刊登期次
1979年				
北京住宅设计竞赛	北京土木建筑学会	524件作品	北京	4
1980年				
全国城市住宅设计竞赛	中国建筑学会和国家建工总局联合主办	7000余件作品	北京	2
1981年				
全国农村住宅设计方案竞赛	国家建委农村房屋建设办公室和中国建筑学会	6500件作品	北京	10
全国中小型剧场设计竞赛	中国建筑学会等	677件作品	北京	3
南京雨花台革命烈士纪念碑建筑设计方案竞赛	南京雨花台烈士陵园管理处	578件作品	江苏	8
1982年				
天津市王顶堤居住区规划设计竞赛	天津市规划局与天津市建筑学会联合举办	不详	天津	11
钓鱼台会议中心设计竞赛	中国建筑学会	8家国内单位	北京	7
1983年				
上海康健新村规划竞赛	上海市城市规划管理局与上海建筑学会	9个方案	上海	6
北京1982年新农村规划设计竞赛	北京土木建筑学会	51个方案	北京	1
浙江五乡集镇规划设计竞赛	浙江省基本建设委员会和浙江省建筑学会	22个方案	浙江	4
吉林省首届农村集镇规划设计竞赛	国家建委同吉林省建委、省建筑学会	18个方案	吉林	4
1984年				
全国村镇规划竞赛	中国建设部	1028件作品	北京	6
全国农村集镇剧场竞赛	城乡建设环境保护部等	129件作品	北京	2
四川自贡恐龙博物馆设计邀请竞赛	四川自贡恐龙博物馆	70件作品	四川	2
河北省科技馆设计竞赛	河北省计委	35件作品	河北	7
1984年建筑学大学生国际竞赛	UIA协会	186件作品	不详	5
首届建筑摄影竞赛	建筑学报	2548件作品	北京	5
日本国际建筑设计竞赛	日本政府	370份作品	日本	5
1985年				
陕西省革命英烈纪念馆设计方案评选	陕西省政府	25件作品	陕西	2
全国村镇建筑竞赛	城乡建设环境保护部	182件作品	北京	11
全国城市中小学建筑设计方案竞赛	教育部	295件作品	南京	3
1987年				
上海市厨房、卫生间设计竞赛	华东地区建筑标准设计协作办公室等	195件作品	上海	1
四川省"七五"期间城镇住宅设计竞赛	四川省政府	不详	四川	7
1988年				
全国文化馆设计竞赛	中国建筑学会	1165件作品	北京	1
北京西单民族大厦方案竞赛	中国建筑学会等	6家国内单位	北京	9
汕头特区珠池区综合中心规划竞赛	中国建筑学会等	不详	广东	12

80

建筑竞赛始终是建筑设计领域的重要组成部分，许多建筑佳作都是由建筑竞赛产生的。建筑竞赛为中国建筑设计事业带来强大的动力，它最大程度地发挥了设计师的创造性，开拓了建筑师的视野，促进了设计师的交流，并在很大程度上促进了中国建筑文化的发展。

Architectural competitions have always been an important part of architecture design. They bring a formidable energy to Chinese architectural design: developing the architectural view, promoting a designer's communication skills, as well as enriching Chinese architectural culture development.

竞赛名称	举办者	参赛作品	举办地	刊登期次
1989年				
北京动物园举办大熊猫馆设计竞赛	北京动物园	10件作品	北京	4
1990年				
深圳商业大厦建筑方案竞赛	深圳华商进出口公司	45件作品	广东	8
1989年全国城镇商品住宅设计竞赛	中国建设部	4000余件作品	北京	5
1991年				
幼儿园建筑设计方案竞赛	中国建筑学会	924件作品	北京	3
1992年				
建筑设计作品大赛	中国建筑学会	438件作品	北京	2
外交部办公大楼方案设计竞赛	外交部	7家国内单位	北京	7
中国"八五"新住宅设计竞赛	建设部设计司与建筑学会	3000件作品	北京	5
1994年				
全国村镇住宅设计大奖赛	中国建设部	135件作品	北京	1
珠海大学规划与建筑国际竞赛	珠海市政府	4家单位	广东	6
湖南省93年商品住宅建筑设计竞赛	湖南省政府	216件作品	湖南	2
1996年				
广西人民大会堂设计竞赛	广西建委	不详	广西	7
第6届国际大学生建筑设计竞赛	美国ACSA/OTIS	2250名学生参加	葡萄牙	6
1997年				
96上海住宅设计国际竞赛	上海市政府	592件作品	上海	3
2000中国小康住宅设计国际竞赛	中国建设部与美国公司联合举办	13家国内外单位	北京	3
96全国大学生建筑设计竞赛	全国高等学校建筑学专业指导委员会	286件作品	西安	2
上海新江湾城（一期）国际竞赛	上海设计招投标办公室	7家单位	上海	11
1998年				
98全球设计挑战赛	美国欧文斯科宁集团	42件作品	美国	11
1999年				
UIA第二十届大会国际建筑专业学生设计竞赛	国际建筑师协会	466件作品	北京	5
首届全国电脑建筑画大赛	中国建筑工业出版社等	532件作品	北京	1
"迈向21世纪的住宅"竞赛	中国建设部	不详	北京	6
福建省迈向21世纪住宅设计竞赛	福建省政府	不详	福建	11
深圳会展中心国际设计竞标	深圳市政府	11家国内外单位	广东	6
2000年				
国家大剧院方案竞赛	国家大剧院工程业主委员会	32家国内外单位	北京	1
国际优秀建筑毕业设计竞赛	国际建筑师协会	不详	俄罗斯	1

建筑竞赛——以《建筑学报》（1978－2006）为例

A COLLECTION OF ARCHITECTURAL COMPETITION BASED ON ARCHITECTURAL JOURNAL(1978-2006)

竞赛名称	举办者	参赛作品	举办地	刊登期次
2001年				
北京国际展览体育中心竞赛	北京市政府	16家国内外单位	北京	1
浙江大学新校园(基础部)概念性规划设计竞赛	浙江大学	67份作品	浙江	5
1999－2000ACSA/OTIS国际学生竞赛	美国ACSA/OTIS	1245名学生参加	香港	1
2002年				
首届中国绿色生态住宅设计大赛	中国建筑学会	149件	北京	8
亚澳地区国际大学生建筑创作设计竞赛	中国建筑学会和国际建协《北京之路》工作组	170件作品	北京	1
惠普杯全国青少年活动场所设计竞赛	全国青少年校外教育工作联席会议办公室	425件作品	北京	9
2000－2001ACSA/OTIS国际学生竞赛	美国ACSA/OTIS	500余件作品	土耳其	6
2003年				
2002年全国经济适用房方案竞赛	中国建筑学会	453件作品	北京	3
南京仙林大学城中心区城市设计国际竞赛	南京仙林大学	不详	南京	11
国家体育场建筑概念设计方案竞赛	中国政府	14家单位	北京	5
国家游泳馆中心建筑设计竞赛	北京市规划委员会	10家国内外单位	北京	8
国家图书馆二期设计方案		9家国内外单位	北京	10
徐州新区起步区规划设计国际方案竞赛	中国建筑学会、徐州市政府	6家单位	徐州	
2004年				
广州新城市中轴线电视观光塔设计竞赛	广州市政府	14家国内外单位	广州	10
首都国际机场3号航站楼竞赛	中国政府	7家国内外单位	北京	6
国家网球中心及国家曲棍球场建筑设计方案竞赛	国家网球中心及国家曲棍球场建设管理委员会	8家国内外单位	北京	7
上海市郊区村民住宅设计竞赛	上海市政府	不详	上海	10
中关村国际生命医疗园修建性详细规划设计竞赛	北京中关村生命科学园发展有限责任公司	5家国内外单位	北京	8
首届全国高速公路附属设施方案设计竞赛	中国建筑学会	不详	北京	6
"城市庆典"概念设计竞赛	国际建筑师协会	不详	德国	3
2005年				
第二届中国威海国际建筑设计大奖赛	中国建筑学会、山东建设厅、威海人民政府	不详	威海	11
第三届DBEW国际住宅设计竞赛	韩国汉森公司	305件作品	韩国	4
2006年				
2006全国建筑院系大学生建筑设计竞赛	中国建筑学会与全国高等学校建筑学科专执委	367件作品	北京	12
首届金地大学生建筑设计大赛	金地集团与《建筑学报》联合主办	113件作品	北京	2
全国首届太阳能建筑设计竞赛	中国太阳能学会与中国建筑学会	87件作品	北京	3
第三届中国威海国际建筑设计大奖赛	中国建筑学会、山东建设厅、威海人民政府	1005件作品	威海	11
宁波太丰面粉厂改造竞赛	宁波规划局	6家国内外单位	浙江	8

表 5-1

从中国近三十年的发展特点看，设计竞赛大致经历了三个阶段：

1978－1989年恢复阶段。为配合国家发展，建设部和建筑学会开展了各种建筑类型的全国性竞赛，掀起了一股热潮，大多是一种探索性的竞赛。

1990－1999年发展阶段。各种实际项目的公开国内外招标竞赛增多，住宅竞赛数量逐渐凸现。此外，中国人在国际设计竞赛中也开始崭露头角。

2000－2006年高潮阶段。随着国民经济的持续发展以及奥运会、世博会的申办成功，一批国家大型建筑设计竞赛展开。众多国内外设计界名家大师参与其中，促使中国建筑发展进入了新的阶段。

Reviewing the recent 30 years of competition development in china, the design competition has approximately experienced three stages:

Recovering phase (1978—1989) - In order to coordinate the national development, the Ministry of Construction and the ASC carried out competitions of various kinds which raised a building growth, most are exploratory competitions;

Developmental phase(1990—1999) - Actual projects open publicly to domestic and foreign competition increased, the quantity of housing competitions improved, Chinese also began taking part in international design competitions.

Climactic phase (2000—2006) - Continues the developmental phase but enters into new stage as the Olympic Games 2008 and World Exposition 2010 along with the burgeoning national economy bring grand national project competitions. The participation of lots architecture masters, both domestic and foreign, promoted Chinese architecture development enters a new phase.

表 5-1 秦臻根据《建筑学报》（1978－2006）整理

图 5-1 《建筑学报》封面：亚澳地区国际大学生建筑创作竞赛二等奖设计方案

国家自然科学奖
NATIONAL NATURAL SCIENCE AWARD

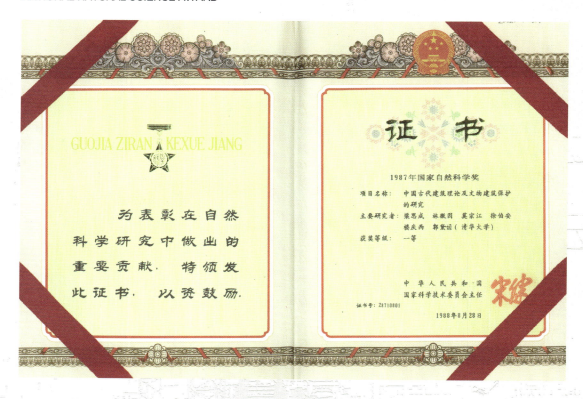

GUOJIA ZIRAN KEXUE JIANG

为表彰在自然科学研究中做出的重要贡献，特颁发此证书，以资鼓励.

证 书

1987年国家自然科学奖

项目名称： 中国古代建筑理论及文物建筑保护的研究
主要研究者： 梁思成 林徽因 莫宗江 徐伯安 楼庆西 郭黛姮（清华大学）
获奖等级： 一等

中 华 人 民 共 和 · 国
国家科学技术委员会主任 宋健

证书号： Z8710801

1988年8月28日

图 6-1 梁思成等获 1987 年国家自然科学奖一等奖

国家自然科学奖是标志中国科学技术水平的最高奖项，专门授予在基础研究和应用基础研究中阐明自然现象、特征和规律，做出重大科学发现的科技工作者。

The National Natural Science Prize is the award which marks the highest level of science and technology in China, specially authorized to scientific experts who make great scientific discovery in expounding natural phenomena, characteristics and laws in fundamental research.

6 中国建筑奖项
ARCHITECTURE AWARDS OF CHINA

梁思成奖
LIANG SICHENG ARCHITECTURE PRIZE

2000年	第一届中国建筑学会梁思成建筑奖获奖人员（9名）	
	齐　康	东南大学建筑学院
	莫伯治	广州市城市规划局
	赵冬日	北京市建筑设计研究院
	关肇邺	清华大学建筑学院
	魏敦山	上海现代建筑设计（集团）有限公司
	张锦秋	中国建筑西北设计研究院
	何镜堂	华南理工大学建筑设计研究院
	张开济	北京市建筑设计研究院
	吴良镛	清华大学建筑学院
2002年	第二届中国建筑学会梁思成建筑奖获奖人员（2名）	
	马国馨	北京市建筑设计研究院
	彭一刚	天津大学建筑学院
2004年	第三届中国建筑学会梁思成建筑奖获奖人员（1名）	
	程泰宁	中国联合工程公司
2006年	第四届中国建筑学会梁思成建筑奖获奖人员（2名）	
	王小东	新疆建筑设计研究院
	崔　恺	中国建筑设计研究院

表 6-1

梁思成建筑奖是由中华人民共和国建设部设立的，授予本国建筑师的最高荣誉奖。2000 年进行了首届的评选和颁奖。自 2001 年起，本奖每两年评选一次，每次设梁思成建筑奖 2 名，梁思成建筑提名奖 2 至 4 名。

The Liang Sicheng Architecture Prize, established by the Ministry of Construction in the People's Republic of China, is an architect's highest honor. In 2000 the first session of evaluation and first award ceremony were held. From 2001, this prize is awarded every two years to two architects from two to four nominees.

表 6-1 秦臻绘制 资料来源：中国建筑学会网站.[EB/OL]，2006.[2007-02-07].
http://www.chinaasc.org/zt/hjbz/lscjzj.php

中国建筑学会建筑教育奖
ARCHITECTURAL EDUCATION AWARD OF ASC

2004年	第一届中国建筑学会建筑教育奖获奖人员（2名）	
	齐 康	东南大学建筑研究所
	鲍家声	南京大学建筑研究所
	第一届中国建筑学会建筑教育特别奖获奖人员（5名）	
	冯纪忠	同济大学建筑与城市规划学院
	吴良镛	清华大学建筑与城市研究所
	唐 璞	重庆大学建筑学院
	张钦楠	中国建筑学会
	林 宣	西安建筑科技大学建筑学院
2006年	第二届中国建筑学会建筑教育奖获奖人员（3名）	
	彭一刚	天津大学建筑学院
	秦佑国	清华大学建筑学院
	李德华	同济大学建筑学院
	第二届中国建筑学会建筑教育特别奖获奖人员（9名）	
	罗小未	同济大学建筑学院
	高亦兰	清华大学建筑学院
	蔡镇钰	上海现代建筑设计集团公司
	聂兰生	天津大学建筑学院
	刘先觉	东南大学建筑学院
	梅季魁	哈尔滨工业大学建筑学院
	张似赞	西安建筑科技大学建筑学院
	陈志华	清华大学建筑学院
	陈启高	重庆大学建筑学院

表 6-2

The Architectural Education Award of ASC was established to recognize those architectural educators who have made significant contributions to architectural education and those who have gone a long way to promote the cause of architectural education. The award comes in two categories: one is "The Architectural Education Award of ASC," which represents the highest honor an architectural educator can ever receive, and the other is "The Special Architectural Education Award of ASC", which is given to senior architectural educators and non-professionals who have made important contributions to architectural education. Established in 2004, the award is given once every two years.

中国建筑学会建筑教育奖，旨在表彰在建筑教育方面作出重大贡献的建筑教育工作者和对建筑教育事业起过重大推动作用的人士。奖项分为两个等级：一是"中国建筑学会建筑教育奖"，该奖是授予我国建筑教育工作者的最高荣誉奖；二是"中国建筑学会建筑教育特别奖"，该奖授予杰出的资深建筑教育家及对建筑教育作出重大贡献的非专业人士。该奖项自 2004 年设立，每两年评选一次。

表 6-2 秦臻绘制 资料来源：中国建筑学会网站. [EB/OL] ，2006. [2007-02-07]. http://www.chinaasc.org/zt/hjbz/jzjy.php
文字部分来源：第二届中国建筑学会建筑教育奖. [J].建筑学报，2006 年第九期

中国建筑学会建筑创作奖
ARCHITECTURE CREATION AWARD OF ASC

	获奖项目	设计单位	设计者
1993年	首届中国建筑学会建筑创作奖获奖项目		
	1953—1988年（共计62项）：		
	50—70年代：略		
	1980-1987年（28项）：		
	白天鹅宾馆	广州市建筑设计院	余畯南、黄伯治、林兆璋
	鉴真纪念堂	清华大学建筑系	梁思成、莫宗江、张致中
	武夷山庄	南京工学院建筑研究所等	齐 康等
	龙柏饭店	华东建筑设计研究院	倪天增、张乾源等
	拉萨饭店	江苏省建筑设计院	陆宗лю、赵复兴
	阙里宾舍	建设部建筑设计院	戴念慈等
	国际展览中心	北京市建筑设计研究院	柴裴义、张天纯等
	北京图书馆新馆	建设部建筑设计院等	杨廷宝等
	国际饭店	建设部建筑设计院	林乐义、蒋仲均等
	自贡恐龙博物馆	中国西南建筑设计院	高士策、夏朗风、吴德富等
	天河体育中心	广州市建筑设计院	郭明卓、余兆宋等
	北京昆仑饭店	北京市建筑设计研究院	熊 明、寿振华、刘 刀等
	深圳体育馆	建设部建筑设计院	熊承新、梁应添等
	松江方塔园	同济大学建筑系	冯纪忠等
	天津大学建筑系馆	天津大学建筑设计研究院	彭一刚等
	深圳南海酒店	建设部建筑设计院华森建筑与工程顾问设计公司	陈世民、谢明星
	黄鹤楼	湖北省建筑设计研究院	向欣然等
	沈阳机器人示范工程中心试验楼	中国建筑东北设计院	任焕章、黄良平等
	杭州黄龙饭店	杭州市建筑设计院	程泰宁、胡岩良、徐东平等
	华东电业管理大楼	华东建筑设计研究院	魏志达、王 时等
	缙云电影院	同济大学建筑设计院	葛如亮等
	中美上海施贵宝制药有限公司	华东建筑设计研究院	陈雪莉、苏肇瑜等
	侵华日军南京大屠杀遇难同胞纪念馆	东南大学建筑研究所等	齐 康等
	深圳国际贸易中心	湖北工业建筑设计院	黎卓健、袁培煌等
	无锡沁园新村利居住小区	无锡市建筑设计院	许克勤、王志杰等
	埃及开罗会议中心	上海建筑设计研究院	魏敦山、滕 典等
	新疆人民会堂	新疆建筑设计院	孙国城、韩布琛、王小东等
	肯尼亚体育中心	中国西南建筑设计院	周方中、吴德富等
	1988—1992年（共计8项）：		
	清华大学图书馆新馆	清华大学建筑设计院	关肇邺、叶茂煦、郑金床等
	北京菊儿胡同新四合院住宅工程	清华大学建筑设计院	吴良镛、卢连生、刘文杰等
	深圳华夏艺术中心	建设部建筑设计院华森建筑与工程顾问设计公司	张孚佩、周 平、曾 筠
	深圳大学演艺会场	深圳大学建筑设计研究院	梁鸿文、陈崇德等
	陕西省历史博物馆	西北建筑设计院	张锦秋、王天星等
	广州西汉南越王墓博物馆	华南理工大学建筑设计院	莫伯治、何镜堂、李绮霞等
	北京国家奥林匹克体育中心	北京市建筑设计研究院	马国馨等
	南京梅园周恩来纪念馆	东南大学建筑设计院	齐 康、许立立、曹斌等

"中国建筑学会建筑创作奖"是建筑创作优秀成果的最高荣誉奖之一，旨在鼓励中国建筑师的独创精神和表彰优秀作品。该奖项设立于1992年，2004年开始每两年举办一次，奖项分为"中国建筑学会建筑创作优秀奖"和"建筑创作佳作奖"两个等级，主要表彰获得建筑创作优秀和佳作奖的工作项目、设计单位和主要创作人员。

The Architecture Creation Award of ASC, one of the highest honor for the outstanding architectural innovation projects, is meant to encourage Chinese architects' innovative spirit while recognizing the excellent works. Set up in 1992, the award has been given once every two years since 2004. Provided in two categories, "The Excellent Award for Architectural Creation" and "The Good Work Award for Architectural Creation", the award recognizes the winning projects, design units, and chief innovating personnel.

表 6-3 秦臻绘制 资料来源：中国建筑学会网站.[EB/OL]．2006.
[2007-02-07]. http://www.chinaasc.org/zt/hjbz/jzccj.php
文字部分来源：第四届中国建筑学会建筑创作奖．[J].建筑学报，第 12 届亚洲建筑史大会专集

	获奖项目	设计单位	设计者
1996年	**第二届中国建筑学会建筑创作奖获奖项目**		
	优秀奖（9项）：		
	"东方明珠"上海广播电视塔	华东建筑设计研究院	凌本立、项祖荃、张秀林
	甲午海战馆	天津大学建筑设计研究院	彭一刚、张 华、马奎祥
	恩济里小区	北京市建筑设计研究院	白德懋、叶谋兆、刘晓钟
	上海博物馆	上海建筑设计研究院	邢同和、滕 典、杨洁清
	炎黄艺术馆	北京市建筑设计研究院	刘 力、郭明华、周文瑶
	黑龙江速滑馆	哈尔滨工业大学建筑设计研究院	梅季魁、王奎仁、孙晓鹤
	加纳国家剧院	杭州市建筑设计院	程泰宁、叶湘菌、蒋淑仙
	中国华录电子有限公司	中国电子工程设计院	黄星元、侯海宝、周景溪
	汕头市委办公楼	广东省建筑设计研究院	郭怡昌、蔡斐丽
	提名奖（18项）：略		
2004年	**第三届中国建筑学会建筑创作奖获奖项目**		
	优秀奖（14项）：		
	新疆国际大巴扎	新疆建筑设计研究院	王小东等
	北京钓鱼台国宾馆芳菲苑	同济大学建筑设计研究院	曾 群、孙 晔
	外语教学与研究出版社办公楼	中旭建筑设计有限责任公司	崔 恺、郑 雪、王 祎
	三亚喜来登酒店	北京市建筑设计研究院	金卫钧、张 耕、孙 勃
	孟中友谊国际会议中心	北京市建筑设计研究院	柴裴义、叶依谦、耿 炜
	北京首都国际机场扩建工程新航站楼	北京市建筑设计研究院	马国馨、马 丽、王 兵
	黄帝陵祭祀大院（殿）工程	中国建筑西北设计研究院	张锦秋、高朝君、陈初聚
	上海图书馆	上海建筑设计研究院有限公司	张皆正、唐玉恩、居其宏
	海南海口火车站	中元国际工程设计研究院	王长刚、曹亮功、谢新平
	北京现代城A区（SOHO现代城）	北京市建筑设计研究院	朱小地、贾更生、谢 强
	深圳国际技术创新研究院研发大楼	中建国际（深圳）设计顾问有限公司	沈立众、单增亮、王俊东
	浙江省舟山市沈家门小学	天津大学建筑设计研究院	彭一刚、杨淑玲、汪丽君
	富凯大厦	中国建筑设计研究院	崔 恺、崔海东、张 波
	同济大学中德学院大楼	同济大学建筑设计研究院	庄 慎、胡 茸、张洛先
	佳作奖（26项）：略		
2006年	**第四届中国建筑学会建筑创作奖获奖项目**		
	优秀奖（15项）：		
	河南安阳殷墟博物馆	中国建筑设计研究院	崔 恺、张 男
	中国美术学院整体改造工程	北京市建筑设计研究院	李承德、杜 松、马红文
	清华大学附小新校舍	清华大学建筑学院等	王丽方、马学聪、陈 伟
	山东曲阜孔子研究院工程	清华大学建筑设计研究院	吴良镛等
	西藏博物馆主馆	中国建筑西南设计研究院	赵擎夏、刘 军、聂 毅
	中国科学院图书馆	中科建筑设计研究院有限责任公司	崔 彤、白小青、高 林
	中国南通珠算博物馆	上海兴田建筑工程设计事务所	王兴田、杜富存、黄 震
	苏州规划展示馆	苏州市建筑设计研究院有限责任公司	宋希民、顾柏男、蔡 爽
	广州大学城广东药学院教学区	华南理工大学建筑设计研究院	何镜堂等
	北京大学国际关系学院	北京市建筑设计研究院	褚 平、查世旭
	中软昌平总部大楼	中国建筑设计研究院	曹晓昕、孙 雷
	南京森林公安高等专科学校主体建筑群	东南大学建筑设计研究院	韩冬青等
	博鳌BFA索菲特酒店及会议中心	北京市建筑设计研究院	杜 松、张 宇
	联想研发基地	北京市建筑设计研究院	谢 强、吴剑利、金卫钧
	联想园区C座	北京市建筑设计研究院	陈淑慧、金卫钧、谢中午
	佳作奖（31项）：略		

表 6-3

89

中国建筑学会青年建筑师奖
YOUNG ARCHITECT AWARDS OF ASC

1993年	中国建筑学会青年建筑师奖（试行）获奖者名单		宋海林	清华大学建筑设计研究院
	庄惟敏	清华大学建筑设计院	周 凌	南京大学建筑研究所
	张俊杰	上海华东建筑设计院	郭卫宏	华南理工大学建筑设计研究院
	宋 源	建设部建筑设计院	柴培根	中国建筑设计研究院
1994年	第一届中国建筑学会青年建筑师奖获奖者名单		谢 强	北京市建筑设计研究院
	王 蕃	建设部建筑技术发展中心	曾笑钢	中元国际工程设计研究院
	宋 源	建设部建筑设计院	王 戈	北京市建筑设计研究院
1995年	第二届中国建筑学会青年建筑师奖获奖者名单		王文胜	同济大学建筑设计研究院
	优秀奖：		吴 杰	同济大学建筑设计研究院
	王绍森	合肥工大建筑学系	李兴钢	中国建筑设计研究院
	陈一峰	清华大学建筑设计研究院	崔海东	中国建筑设计研究院
	吴 越	深圳华森公司	王 军	中国建筑设计西北设计研究院
	朱小地	北京市建筑设计研究院	刘 淼	北京市建筑设计研究院
	林怀文	清华大学建筑设计研究院	杨易栋	浙江大学建筑设计研究院
	杨 瑛	湖南省建筑设计院	朱 明	广东省高教建筑规划设计院
	吴永发	合肥工业大学建筑设计研究院	徐全胜	北京市建筑设计研究院
	邬 健	中南建筑设计院	曲 冰	哈尔滨工业大学建筑设计研究院
	陈 民	北京市建筑设计院		
1997年	第三届中国建筑学会青年建筑师奖获奖者名单	2006年	第六届中国建筑学会青年建筑师奖获奖者名单	
	优秀奖：		王 伟	中国美术学院风景建筑设计研究院
	安庆东	上海建筑设计研究院	文 兵	中国建筑设计研究院
	周春雨	华侨大学建筑系	汤朝晖	华南理工大学建筑设计研究院
	金卫钧	北京市建筑设计研究院	张 男	中国建筑设计研究院
	丁 杰	中国建筑技术研究院	宋晔皓	清华大学建筑学院
	杨 瑛	湖南省建筑设计研究院	李麟学	同济大学建筑与城市规划学院
	马 涛	辽宁省建筑设计研究院	高庆辉	东南大学建筑设计研究院
	周红雷	江苏省建筑设计研究院	凌克戈	华东建筑设计研究院有限公司
	吴学俊	湖南省建筑设计研究院	鲁 丹	浙江大学建筑设计研究院
	马慧超	同济大学建筑设计研究院	吕 舟	中元国际工程设计研究院
1998年	第四届中国建筑学会青年建筑师奖获奖者名单		戎武杰	上海现代建筑设计（集团）有限公司现代都市建筑设计院
	优秀奖：		张 彤	东南大学建筑学院
	王 昕	华森建筑与工程设计顾问有限公司	谷 建	中元国际工程设计研究院
	许 迪	华南理工大学建筑设计研究院	吴 晨	北京市建筑设计研究院
	陈 光	北京市建筑设计研究院	肖 蓝	华森建筑与工程设计顾问有限公司
	杨晓川	华南理工大学建筑设计研究院	赵劲松	天津大学建筑学院
	解 钧	北京市建筑设计研究院	秦 峰	中国建筑设计西北设计研究院
	冼剑雄	华南理工大学建筑设计研究院	傅绍辉	中国航空工业规划设计研究院
	杨 晔	辽宁省建筑设计院	叶 彪	清华大学建筑设计研究院
2004年	第五届中国建筑学会青年建筑师奖获奖者名单		付本臣	哈尔滨工业大学建筑设计研究院
	王 玮	中旭建筑设计有限责任公司	刘 艺	中国建筑设计西南设计研究院
	叶长青	浙江大学建筑设计研究院	朱铁麟	天津市建筑设计院
	卢志刚	华东建筑设计研究院有限公司	杜 松	北京市建筑设计研究院
	叶依谦	北京市建筑设计研究院	张 斌	同济大学建筑设计研究院
	刘 斌	中国建筑西北设计研究院四所	陈 缨	华东建筑设计研究院有限公司
	祁 斌	清华大学建筑设计研究院	李亦农	北京市建筑设计研究院
	刘宇波	华南理工大学建筑设计研究院	陆晓明	中信武汉市建筑设计院
			黄 勇	哈尔滨工业大学建筑学院

表 6-4

中国建筑学会青年建筑师奖为设计领域中中国青年建筑师的最高荣誉奖，旨在表彰在建筑设计中作出突出成就的青年建筑师。该奖每两年举办一次，每次奖励人数不超过 30 名。申报人必须从事建筑设计工作 3 年以上，年龄在 25 至 40 周岁内。

The Young Architect Award of ASC, the highest honor given to a young architect engaged in the area of design, aims to recognize the young architects who have accomplished great achievement in architectural design. The award, launched once every two years, is given to no more than 30 candidates at a time. Anyone applying for the award should be aged between 25 to 40, with at least three years working experience in architectural design.

随着建筑设计的发展，各种杂志类奖项也开始出现，其中较为突出的有《世界建筑》杂志主办的 WA 中国建筑奖，从 2002 年至今已成功的举办了三次，影响力越来越大。

Along with the development of architectural design, various kinds of awards established by magazines also emerged. WA Chinese Architecture Award sponsored by *World Architecture* is one prominent example. Since 2002 the prize has been successfully held three times and has increased its influence.

表 6-4 秦臻绘制 资料来源：中国建筑学会网站.[EB/OL]，2006.[2007-02-07].
http://www.chinaasc.com/zt/hjbz/qnjzsj.php
青年建筑师奖部分文字来源：第六届中国建筑学会青年建筑师奖揭晓.[J].建筑学报，第 12 届亚洲建筑史大会专集

联合国"世界人居奖"
WORLD HABITAT AWARD OF UNITED NATIONS
图 6-2 清华大学吴良镛教授设计的菊儿胡同获联合国"世界人居奖"

图 6-2 资料来源：秦泰阳．《城市·建筑》[M]．北京，2000：104

图片来源：陈瑶截改绘。资料来源：张耀 摄.奥运村工地塔吊叠画集
[EB/OL].北京：北京日报,2006(2006-08-02)[2007-02-07].
http://epaper.bjd.com.cn/rb/20060802/200608/t20060802_60226.htm

7 中国建筑院校
ARCHITECTURE SCHOOLS OF CHINA

建筑院校分布
DISTRIBUTION OF ARCHITECTURE SCHOOLS OF CHINA

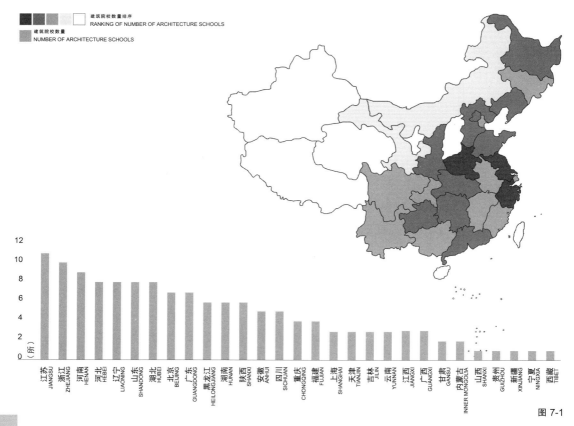

建筑院校数量排序
RANKING OF NUMBER OF ARCHITECTURE SCHOOLS

建筑院校数量
NUMBER OF ARCHITECTURE SCHOOLS

图 7-1

20世纪 90 年代以来，中国建筑院校在数量上大幅度增加，从 20 世纪 80 年代的 30 余个发展到今天的 170 余个。

从分布范围来看，建筑院校大致集中在建筑市场较发达地区，且大部分院校在直辖市、省会城市或特区。西部地区建筑教育相对薄弱。

Since the 1990's, the number of architecture schools in China has increased very fast, from more than 30 in the 1980's to over 170 currently.

The range of distribution depicts architecture schools concentrating on the developed area of the architecture market. Most are in municipality, provincial capitals or special zones. The state of architecture education in the western region is not so well developed comparably.

图 7-1 秦臻根据各建筑院校网站信息绘制

图 7-2　清华大学建筑学院专业教室

国内主要建筑院校
MAJOR ARCHITECTURE SCHOOLS

主要建筑院校专业设置

学校名称	本科专业	研究生专业
清华大学建筑学院	建筑学、建筑环境与设备工程	建筑历史与理论，建筑设计及其理论，城市规划与设计，景观建筑学，建筑技术科学，供热、燃气、通风及空调工程；艺术学
同济大学建筑与城市规划学院	建筑学、城市规划、历史建筑保护工程、工业设计、艺术设计、旅游规划、景观规划设计	建筑历史与理论，建筑设计及其理论，城市规划与设计，建筑技术科学，景观规划设计；设计艺术学
东南大学建筑学院	建筑学、城市规划和艺术设计	建筑历史与理论，建筑设计及其理论，城市规划与设计，景观建筑学，建筑技术科学，建筑遗产保护与管理；美术学
天津大学建筑学院	建筑学、城市规划和环境艺术	建筑历史与理论，建筑设计及其理论，城市规划与设计，建筑技术科学，建筑环境设计；美术学，设计艺术学，艺术学
重庆大学建筑学院	建筑学、城市规划	建筑历史与理论，建筑设计及其理论，城市规划与设计，景观建筑学，建筑技术科学，室内设计；设计艺术学
哈尔滨工业大学建筑学院	建筑学、城市规划和艺术设计	建筑历史与理论，建筑设计及其理论，城市规划与设计，建筑技术科学
西安建筑科技大学建筑学院	建筑学、城市规划和艺术设计	建筑历史与理论，建筑设计及其理论，城市规划与设计，建筑技术科学
华南理工大学建筑学院	建筑学、城市规划、景观设计	建筑设计及其理论，城市规划与设计，建筑技术科学，景观建筑学；岩土工程，结构工程，市政工程，供热、燃气、通风及空调工程，防灾减灾工程及防护工程，桥梁与隧道工程，水力学及河流动力学，工程力学

主要建筑院校概览

表 7-1

清华大学建筑系由著名建筑学家梁思成教授创建于 1946 年 10 月。1988 年成立建筑学院。（现任院长朱文一）

东南大学建筑系始建于 1927 年，是中国第一个建筑系。杨廷宝、刘敦桢、童寯教授长期在此执教。曾名南京工学院建筑系，2003 年组建建筑学院。（现任院长王建国）

重庆大学建筑城规学院的前身重庆建筑工程学院建筑系，成立于 1952 年，1994 年学校更名重庆建筑大学，建筑系更名为建筑城规学院。2000 年新重庆大学组建后，更名为重庆大学建筑城规学院。（现任院长张兴国）

西安建筑科技大学建筑系成立于 1956 年，曾名西安冶金学院建筑系，1996 年成立建筑学院。（现任院长刘克成）

同济大学建筑系，成立于 1952 年，1986 年成立建筑与城市规划学院。（现任院长吴志强）

天津大学建筑学专业前身为 1935 年创建的天津工商学院建筑系。1952 年 9 月院系调整后，成立天津大学建筑系。1997 年 6 月成立天津大学建筑学院。（现任院长彭一刚）

哈尔滨工业大学建筑系创建于 1920 年 10 月。1959 年院系调整后成立哈尔滨建筑工程学院建筑系。后改为哈尔滨建筑大学建筑学院。2000 年与哈尔滨工业大学合并，成立哈尔滨工业大学建筑学院。（现任院长张姗姗）

华南理工大学建筑学系创建于 1932 年，1997 年 11 月成立建筑学院。（现任院长何镜堂）

96

20 世纪 50 年代，经过全国范围的院系调整，中国共有八所大学设有建筑系，分别是清华大学、南京工学院（即东南大学）、同济大学、天津大学、华南工学院（即华南理工大学）、重庆建筑工程学院（即重庆大学）、哈尔滨建筑工程学院（即哈尔滨工业大学）、西安冶金建筑学院（即西安建筑科技大学），被称为"建筑八大院校"。今天，这八所建筑院校在中国建筑教育界仍扮演着重要角色。

In the 1950's, through nationwide restructuring of universities, eight universities held architecture departments in China. Tsinghua University, Nanjing Institute of Technology(i.e., Southeast University), Tongji University, Tianjin University, South China Institute of Technology (i.e., South China University of Technology), Chongqing Institute of Civil Engineering & Architecture (i.e., Chongqing University), Harbin Institute of Civil Engineering & Architecture (i.e. ,Harbin Institute of Technology), and the Xi'an Metallurgy Construction College (i.e., Xi'sn University of Architecture &Technology), were called "The Eight Architecture Schools". Today, these eight architecture schools are still playing important roles in the architecture education field.

表 7-1　秦璐根据各学院网站整理

高等学校建筑学及城市规划专业指导委员会
COMMITTEE OF EDUCATIONAL INSTRUCTION OF NATIONAL COLLEGE IN ARCHITECTURE & URBAN PLANNING

高等学校建筑学专业指导委员会（2005.10-2009.10）

主持学校：		
东南大学		
顾　问：（按姓氏笔划排序共4人）		
关肇邺	院士	清华大学
齐　康	院士	东南大学
郑时龄	院士	同济大学
彭一刚	院士	天津大学
主任委员：		
仲德昆	教授	东南大学
副主任委员：（按姓氏笔划排序共4人）		
朱文一	教授	清华大学
吴长福	教授	同济大学
张　颀	教授	天津大学
赵红红	教授	华南理工大学
委　员：（按姓氏笔划排序共28人）		
丁沃沃（女）	教授	南京大学
孔宇航	教授	大连理工大学
仲德昆	教授	东南大学
刘克成	教授	西安建筑科技大学
刘　甦	教授	山东建筑工程学院
刘　塨	教授	华侨大学
朱文一	教授	清华大学
汤羽扬（女）	教授	北京建筑工程学院
吴长福	教授	同济大学
吴庆洲	教授	华南理工大学
张兴国	教授	重庆大学
张成龙	教授	吉林建筑工程学院
张伶伶	教授	哈尔滨工业大学
张　颀	教授	天津大学
李保峰	教授	华中科技大学
沈中伟	教授	西南交通大学
沈　迪	教授级高工	上海现代建筑设计（集团）有限公司
邵韦平	教授级高工	北京市建筑设计研究院
陈伯超	教授	沈阳建筑大学
单　军	教授	清华大学
赵红红	教授	华南理工大学
饶小军	教授	深圳大学
徐　雷	教授	浙江大学
莫天伟	教授	同济大学
崔　恺	教授级高级建筑师	中国建筑设计研究院
韩冬青	教授	东南大学
潘国泰	教授	合肥工业大学
魏春雨	教授	湖南大学

高等学校城市规划专业指导委员会（2005.10-2009.10）

主持学校：		
同济大学		
顾　问：（按姓氏笔划排序共3人）		
吴良镛	院士	清华大学
邹德慈	院士	中国城市规划设计研究院
孟兆祯	院士	北京林业大学
主任委员：		
吴志强	教授	同济大学
副主任委员：（按姓氏笔划排序，共3人）		
毛其智	教授	清华大学
赵万民	教授	重庆大学
顾朝林	教授	南京大学
委　员：（按姓氏笔划排序，共21人）		
王文红	高级工程师	北京市规划委员会
毛其智	教授、	清华大学
石铁矛	教授	沈阳建筑大学
刘博敏	教授	东南大学
华　晨	教授	浙江大学
吕　斌	教授	北京大学
戎　安	教授	北京建筑工程学院
余柏椿	教授	华中科技大学
吴志强	教授	同济大学
张军民	教授	山东建筑工程学院
杨新海	教授	苏州科技学院
肖大威	教授	华南理工大学
运迎霞（女）	教授	天津大学
邱　建	教授	西南交通大学
姜长征	教授级高工	安徽建筑工业学院
赵万民	教授	重庆大学
赵天字	教授	哈尔滨工业大学
赵　民	教授	同济大学
顾朝林	教授	南京大学
黄明华	教授	西安建筑科技大学

表 7-2

In order to raise China's college architecture education level, in May 1989, the Committee of Education Instruction of National College in Architecture was founded. In May 1998, the Committee of Education Instruction of National College in Urban Planning was founded. The two committees, under guidance of the Ministry of Construction , develop the academic curriculum and talent enrichment programs. Their responsibilities are to reform and develop the direction of the academic program as well as to define the direction for the undergraduate and graduate student. Graduate requirements and service structure, course content, academic relations, and teaching material development are also part of the committee's responsibilities.

为提高我国高等学校建筑专业的教育水平，1989 年 5 月全国高等学校建筑学学科专业指导委员会成立。1998 年 5 月全国高等学校城市规划学科专业指导委员会成立。建筑及城市规划学科专业指导委员会是在建设部领导下指导学科建设和人才培养的专家机构。其职责是研究本学科专业教育改革与发展方向，组织制定本学科专业本科生和研究生培养目标，毕业生基本要求和业务规格，教学内容和教学环节基本要求及教材建设等。

表 7-2 秦睿根据以下资料整理 中国建设部人事教育司网站 [EB/OL] ,
http://www.mochr.com/renshi/gaodeng/tujian/mingdan02.asp#1
文字部分主要参考：鲍家声.中国高等学校建筑教育.[J].南方建筑，1997 年第一期

全国高等学校建筑学专业教育评估
EDUCATIONAL ASSESSMENT OF NATIONAL COLLEGE EDUCATION IN ARCHITECTURE

全国高等学校建筑学专业教育评估委员会

第四届全国高等学校建筑学专业教育评估委员会名单
（2003年12月31日通过，任期4年）

主 任 委 员：

秦佑国	教授	清华大学

副主任委员：

王建国	教授	东南大学
曹亮功	教授级高级建筑师	中元国际工程设计研究院

委 员： （20人，按姓氏笔划排序）

王 竹	教授	浙江大学
王伯伟	教授	同济大学
王洪礼	教授级高级建筑师	中国建筑东北设计研究院
孔宇航	教授	大连理工大学
李子萍	教授级高级建筑师	中国建筑西北设计研究院
李志民	教授	西安建筑科技大学
李保峰	教授	华中科技大学
吴英凡	教授级高级建筑师	中国建筑设计研究院
桂学文	教授级高级建筑师	中南建筑设计院
孙一民	教授	华南理工大学
陈梦驹	教授级高级建筑师	华东建设设计研究院
周 畅	教授级高级工程师	中国建筑学会
张玉坤	教授	天津大学
张伶伶	教授	哈尔滨工业大学
唐玉恩	教授级高级建筑师	上海建筑设计研究院
徐行川	教授级高级建筑师	中国建筑西南设计研究院
黄 薇	教授级高级建筑师	北京市建筑设计研究院
梁应添	教授级高级建筑师	北京梁开建筑设计事务所
覃 力	教授	深圳大学
魏宏杨	教授	重庆大学

秘书长： 建设部人事教育司高教处人员担任。

建设部建筑学专业教育评估委员会评估通过并处于有效期内的学校名单（

建筑院系	本科合格有效
清华大学建筑学院建筑系	2004.5-2011.6
同济大学建筑与城市规划学院建筑系	2004.5-2011.6
东南大学建筑学院建筑系	2004.5-2011.6
天津大学建筑学院建筑系	2004.5-2011.6
重庆大学建筑城规学院建筑系	2006.6-2013.6
哈尔滨工业大学建筑学院建筑系（哈建工）	2006.6-2013.6
西安建筑科技大学建筑学院建筑系	2006.6-2013.6
华南理工大学建筑系	2006.6-2013.6
浙江大学建筑工程学院建筑系	2004.5-2011.6
湖南大学建筑学院建筑系	2004.5-2008.6
合肥工业大学建筑与艺术学院建筑系	2004.5-2008.6
北京建筑工程学院建筑系	2004.5-2008.6
深圳大学建筑系	2004.5-2008.6
华侨大学建筑学院建筑系	2004.5-2008.6
北京工业大学建筑与城市规划学院建筑系	2006.6-2010.6
西南交通大学建筑学院建筑系	2006.6-2010.6
华中科技大学建筑与城市规划学院建筑系	2003.6-2007.5
沈阳建筑大学建筑与规划学院建筑系	2003.6-2007.5
郑州大学建筑学院建筑系	2003.6-2007.5
大连理工大学建筑与艺术学院建筑系	2004.5-2008.6
山东建筑大学建筑城规学院建筑系	2004.5-2008.6
昆明理工大学建筑系	2005.6-2009.6
南京工业大学建筑与城市规划学院建筑系	2006.6-2010.6
吉林建筑工程学院建筑系	2006.6-2010.6
武汉理工大学建筑系	2003.6-2007.5
厦门大学建筑系	2003.6-2007.5
广州大学建筑学院	2004.5-2008.6
河北工程大学建筑系	2004.5-2008.6
上海交通大学建筑系	2006.6-2010.6
青岛理工大学建筑系	2006.6-2010.6

表 7-3

98

1989年12月10日由建设部教育司主持在杭州召开全国高等学校建筑学专业教育评估委员会筹备组大会。提出评估委员会由15人组成，其中6名来自高等学校作为建筑教育代表，6名来自设计院作为建筑师代表，其余3名分别来自建设部、国家教委及建筑学会。1990年6月在天津正式成立全国高等学校建筑学专业教育评估委员会，确定15名成员，并首批确定清华大学、同济大学、天津大学和东南大学四校建筑院系进行试点评估工作。

On Dec. 10, 1989, the Education Department of Ministry of Construction hosted the Committee's preparatory congress of Educational Assessment of National College Education in Architecture in Hangzhou. The committee was proposed to be made of 15 persons, 6 coming from the college to act as architecture education representatives, 6 members coming from national design institutes to act as architect representatives, and another 3 members respectively coming from the Ministry of Construction, the State Educational Committee and the ASC. In Jun. 1990, the Committee of Educational Assessment of National College Education in Architecture was set up in Tianjin to be officially made up of 15 members. The first group determined the four schools: Tsinghua University, Tongji University, Tianjin University, and Southeast University, to carry on the assessment duties.

表 7-3 秦臻根据以下资料整理 中国建设部人事教育司官方网站.[EB/OL]，
http://www.mochr.com/renshi/gaodeng/tujian/mingdan02.asp#2

月）

合格有效期	首次通过评估时间	地址	邮编	网址（建筑系或学校网址）
.5-2011.6	1992.5	北京清华园	100084	www.arch.tsinghua.edu.cn
.5-2011.6	1992.5	上海市四平路1239号	200092	www.tongji-caup.org
.5-2011.6	1992.5	南京四牌楼2号	210096	www.arch.seu.edu.cn/
.5-2011.6	1992.5	天津南开区卫津路	300072	202.113.13.67/colleges/architecture/
.6-2013.6	1994.5	重庆市沙坪坝	400045	www.chongjian.com/
.6-2013.6	1994.5	哈尔滨西大直街166号	150001	http://jzxy.hit.edu.cn/
.6-2013.6	1994.5	西安市雁塔路13号	710055	www.xauat.edu.cn/yxsz/jianzhu
.6-2013.6	1994.5	广州市天河区五山	510641	www2.scut.edu.cn/architecture/
.5-2011.6	1996.5	杭州市玉泉浙大路	310027	www.zju.edu.cn/
.5-2008.6	1996.5	长沙市岳麓山	410082	www.jzx.hnu.net.cn/zhu.htm
.5-2008.6	1996.5	合肥市花漾路59号	230009	www1.hfut.edu.cn/department/arch
.5-2008.6	1996.5	北京展览路	100044	www.bicea.edu.cn
	1996.5	深圳市南山区	518060	www.szucace.com
.5-2008.6	1996.5	泉州市东郊	620110	www.info.hqu.edu.cn/jzx/
	1998.5	北京朝阳区平乐园100号	100022	www.bjut.edu.cn/college/arch/xw.htm
.5-2008.6	1998.5	成都市西北桥外九里坡	610031	www.jianzhu.swjtu.edu.cn/
.6-2007.5	1999.5	武汉市武昌珞瑜路	430074	www.hust.edu.cn/chinese/departments
.6-2007.5	1999.5	沈阳市浑南新区	110168	www.sjzu.edu.cn
	1999.5	郑州市大学路	450052	www2.zzu.edu.cn/arch/index.asp
.5-2008.6	2000.5	大连市甘井子凌工路	116023	www.dlut.edu.cn/
	2000.5	济南市和平路47号	250014	www.sdai.edu.cn/
	2001.5	昆明市北环路38号	650093	www.kmustjg.com.cn/
	2002.5	南京市中山北路200号	210009	www.njut.edu.cn/arch/index.htm
	2002.5	长春市红旗街27号	130015	www.jliae.edu.cn
	2003.5	武汉珞狮路122号	430070	www.public.whut.edu.cn/icea/
	2003.5	厦门市思明南路422号	361005	www.archt.xmu.edu.cn/
	2004.5	广州市广园中路248号	510405	www.gzhu.edu.cn/
	2004.5	邯郸市光明南大街199号	56038	www2.hebeu.edu.cn/jianzhu/
	2006.6	上海市华山路口54号	200030	www.arch.sjtu.edu.cn
	2006.6	青岛市抚顺路11号	266033	www.qdiae.edu.cn/

表 7-4

99

In the past two decades, due to the lasting interest in the architecture market and the short supply of architects, architecture study has never been more popular. Many universities have set up architecture departments or urban planning majors. By Jun. of 2006, there were 30 certified schools by the Commission of Educational Assessment of National College Education in Architecture.

近 20 年，由于建筑市场的持续升温，建筑人才供不应求，建筑学成为了社会的热门专业。很多学校纷纷设立建筑学或城市规划专业。截止到 2006 年 6 月，通过建筑学专业教育评估委员会评估通过并处于有效期内的学校共有 30 个。

表 7-4 秦臻根据以下资料整理 中国建设部网站.[EB/OL] ，http://www.cin.gov.cn/edu/pg/2006092801.htm

全国高等学校城市规划专业教育评估
EDUCATIONAL ASSESSMENT OF NATIONAL COLLEGE EDUCATION IN URBAN PLANNING

全国高等学校城市规划专业教育评估委员会

第二届建设部高等教育城市规划专业评估委员会名单
（2003年3月3日通过，任期4年）

主 任 委 员：

赵　民	教授	同济大学

副主任委员：

陈　锋	高级规划师	中国城市规划设计研究院
左　川	教授	清华大学

委　员：　（21人，按姓氏笔划排序）

马武定	教授	厦门市规划局
孔令龙	教授	东南大学
王　君	高级规划师	大连市规划和国土资源局
左　川	教授	清华大学
史小予	高级工程师	广州市城市规划局
石　楠	教授级高级规划师	中国城市规划学会
吕　斌	教授	北京大学
余柏椿	教授	华中科技大学
刑　铭	教授级高级工程师	辽宁省城乡建设规划设计院
陈沧杰	教授级高级工程师	江苏省城乡规划设计研究院
陈　锋	高级规划师	中国城市规划设计研究院
金广君	教授	哈尔滨工业大学
周庆华	教授	西安建筑科技大学
周茂新	教授级高级工程师	浙江省城乡规划设计研究院
施卫良	高级工程师	北京市城市规划设计研究院
赵万民	教授	重庆大学
赵　民	教授	同济大学
夏　青	教授	天津大学
顾朝林	教授	南京大学
蒋宗健	高级工程师	上海市城市规划管理局
魏清泉	教授	中山大学

秘书长：建设部人事教育司高教处人员担任。

建设部城市规划专业教育评估委员会评估通过并处于有效期内的院系名单

城市规划院系	本科合格有效期
清华大学建筑学院城市规划专业（硕士）	
东南大学建筑学院城市规划系	2004.6—2010.
同济大学建筑与城市规划学院城市规划系	2004.5—2010.
重庆大学建筑城规学院城市规划系	2004.5—2010.
哈尔滨工业大学建筑学院城市规划系	2004.5—2010.
天津大学建筑学院城市规划系	2004.6—2010.
西安建筑科技大学建筑学院城市规划系	2006.6—2012.
华中科技大学建筑与城市规划学院城市规划系	2006.6—2012.
南京大学建筑学院城市规划系	2002.7—2006.
华南理工大学城市规划系	2004.6—2008.
山东建筑大学建筑城规学院城市规划系	2004.6—2008.
西南交通大学建筑学院城市规划系	2006.6—2010.
浙江大学建筑工程学院城市规划系	2006.6—2010.

表 7-5

鉴于城市规划学科的发展，1998年高等教育城市规划专业评估委员会成立。成立之初，全国设置城市规划专业的院校不足30个，今天已增至100多个。

The Commission of Educational Assessment of National College Education in Urban Planning was established in Aug. 1998. Because of the development of urban planning, at the beginning of its founding, there were less than 30 schools of urban planning, while there are more than 100 up to now.

表 7-5　秦颖根据以下资料整理 中国建设部人事教育司网站.[EB/OL]，
http://www.mochr.com/renshi/gaodeng/pinggu/pinggu02.asp

合格有效期	首次通过评估时间	地址	邮编	网址（建筑系或学校网址）
.6—2010.6	1998.6	北京清华园	100084	www.arch.tsinghua.edu.cn
.6—2010.6	1998.6	南京四牌楼2号	210096	www.arch.seu.edu.cn/
.5—2010.6	1998.6	上海市四平路1239号	200092	www.tongji-caup.org
.5—2010.6	1998.6	重庆市沙坪坝	400045	www.chongjian.com/
.5—2010.6	1998.6	哈尔滨西大直街166号	150001	http://jzxy.hit.edu.cn/
.6—2012.6	2000.6	天津南开区卫津路	300072	202.113.13.67/colleges/architecture/
.6—2012.6	2000.6	西安市雁塔路13号	710055	www.xauat.edu.cn/yxsz/jianzhu
.6—2012.6	本科2000.6/硕士2006.6	武汉市武昌珞瑜路	430074	www.hust.edu.cn/chinese/departments
.7—2006.6	2002.7	南京市汉口路22号	210093	www.gsa.nju.edu.cn/
.7—2008.6	2002.6	广州市天河区五山	510641	www2.scut.edu.cn/architecture/
	2004.6	济南市和平路47号	250014	www.sdai.edu.cn/
	2006.6	成都市西北桥外九里坡	610031	www.jianzhu.swjtu.edu.cn/
	2006.6	杭州市玉泉浙大路	310027	www.zju.edu.cn/

表 7-6

By Jun. of 2006, there were 13 schools have passed the assessment by the Commission of Educational Assessment of National College Education in Urban Planning and still in period of validity.

截止到 2006 年 6 月，通过城市规划专业教育评估委员会评估通过并处于有效期内的学校共有 13 个。

表 7-6 秦臻根据以下资料整理 中国建设部网站 .[EB/OL]，
http://www.cin.gov.cn/edu/pg/2006092801.htm

后记

——"建筑三书"

　　积累了 20 余年对建筑的兴趣和思考，2006 年 2 月，我开始筹划"建筑三书"，设想从理念设计、建筑现象和空间形式三个方面或三种角度解读建筑，探索建筑的现况与未来走向。第一本书《盖塔·百年联合国——联合国特别纪念日博物馆构想》以意大利古镇盖塔为研究对象，结合重大事件进行建筑与城市设计，已于 2006 年 10 月由清华大学出版社出版发行。第二本书《当代中国建筑图语》以当今世界最大的建设工地——中国为案例梳理建筑现象。而第三本书《第五季空间》（暂定名）则以当下已经出现的、可能预示未来的视觉信息预测未来人类生存空间形式，已于 2007 年 2 月启动，计划于 2007 年底出版。三本书各自独立，又相互关联，形成系列。

　　第一本书《盖塔·百年联合国——联合国特别纪念日博物馆构想》关注城市活力的激发与创造，以意大利古镇盖塔为样本，联合国特别纪念日为线索，构想 2045 年联合国成立 100 周年时，盖塔古镇成为一座展示人类社会发展历程的"博物馆"。由我和黄鹤博士以及陈宇琳、陈瑾羲两位博士研究生组成的研究小组与罗马大学 Monti 教授率领的团队进行合作研究。

　　第二本书《当代中国建筑图语》，尝试通过大量查阅反映当代中国建筑状况的资料和数据，以创造性的"图语"方式直观呈现当代中国建筑状况。本书由"中国建筑发展轨迹"、"中国与世界建筑"、"中国建设量与法规"、"中国设计机构"、"中国建筑媒体"、"中国建筑竞赛"、"中国建筑奖项"、"中国建筑院校"等板块组成，于 2006 年 8 月正式启动。我带领王辉、金秋野、滕静茹、陈宇琳、陈瑾羲和秦臻六位博士研究生利用茶余饭后的时间开展研究。经过不断探索和调整，尤其是后一阶段陈瑾羲、秦臻和我三人的日夜奋战，逐渐形成本书现在的架构和表现形式。

　　需要说明的是，王辉、陈宇琳、金秋野和滕静茹先后参与了本书的部分工作。书中英文部分由陈瑾羲和秦臻翻译，廖炳耀先生校核。在此，对他们为本书所做的工作表示感谢。同时还要感谢清华大学出版社对本书的大力支持，以及邹永华编辑为本书提出的宝贵意见，还有李嫚编辑为本书的后期所做的工作。

朱文一
02/15/2007 于清华园

AFTERWORD

THREE BOOKS ON ARCHITECTURE

After more than 20 years of accumulation of interests and thoughts on architecture, in Feb. 2006, I started to plan for "Three Books on Architecture", attempting to interpret architecture from three different aspects or points, of ideal design, architecture phenomenon and spatial form, to explore the current status of architecture and its future. The first book "*Gaeta: A Celebration of the 100th Anniversary of UN*" was a research study on architecture and urban design with mega-event at an Italian historic town Gaeta, has been published by Tsinghua University Press in Oct. 2006. The second book "*Discourse on the Contemporary Architecture of China*" is a study of the world's largest construction site-China as a case to sort the architecture phenomenon, while the third book "*The Space for the Fifth Season*" (temporary name) will base on some currently emerged visual information, which might predict a future form of human habitation space, has been launched since Feb. 2007, will be published at the end of 2007. The three books are independent but relative.

The first book "*Gaeta: A Celebration of the 100th Anniversary of UN—The Concept of the United Nations Special Days Museum*" is concerned with the stimulation and creation of city vitality. The Italian historic town of Gaeta was taken as a case study. Informed by the UN Special Days museum program, imaged in the future year of 2045, at the 100th anniversary of the founding of the UN, Gaeta would become a "Museum" to display the development process of human society. The research group composed of I, Dr. Huang He, doctoral students Chen Yulin and Chen Jinxi, collaborated with another team at the University of Rome led by Prof. Monti worked together.

The second book *Discourse on the Contemporary Architecture of China*, attempts to refer to a large amount of information and a large number of data, which reflect the state of contemporary architecture in China, to display the current architecture status of China intuitionally with the creative way of "diagram". The book is composed of parts of "Major Architecure Events in China", "China's Position in World's Architecture", "Construction Statistics of China", "Architecture Design

Infrastructures of China", "Architecture Media of China", "Architecture Competitions of China", "Architecture Awards of China" and "Architecture Schools of China", launched in Aug. 2006. I led doctorial students Wang Hui, Jin Qiuye, Teng Jingru, Chen Yulin, Chen Jinxi and Qin Zhen started research at leisure time. With the continuous exploration and adjustment, especially the last moment of working days by Chen Jinxi, Qin Zhen and I, gradually formed the structure and expression of the current book.

It is important to point out that, Wang Hui, Chen Yulin, Jin Qiuye and Teng Jingru took part in part work of the book, Chen Jinxi and Qin Zhen translated it into English and Ben Liao checked the English part of the book. Hereby, thanks for their effort on the book. At the mean time, special thanks will be offered to Tsinghua University Press, to Mr. Zou Yonghua and Ms. Li Man, for their support and invaluable suggestions.

Zhu Wenyi
Feb.15, 2007,Tsinghua University

内 容 简 介

　　本书广泛查阅并引用了大量可靠数据及资料，以创造性的"图语"表达方式反映当代中国建筑状况（不包括港、澳、台资料）。主要内容包括中国建筑发展轨迹、中国与世界建筑、中国建设量与法规、中国设计机构、中国建筑媒体、中国建筑竞赛、中国建筑奖项和中国建筑院校八个部分。

　　本书适用于建筑学及相关专业领域，可供广大关注当代中国建筑状况的读者参考。

图书在版编目（CIP）数据

当代中国建筑图语/朱文一等编著 . —北京：清华大学出版社，2007.6
ISBN 978-7-302-15195-1

Ⅰ . 当…　　Ⅱ . 朱…　　Ⅲ . 建筑业－概况－中国－现代－图集　　Ⅳ . F426.9-64

中国版本图书馆 CIP 数据核字（2007）第 069516 号

责任编辑：邹永华　　李　嫚
封面设计：朱文一
装帧设计：陈瑾羲　　秦　臻
责任校对：王淑云
责任印制：孟凡玉
出版发行：清华大学出版社　　　　地　　　址：北京清华大学学研大厦 A 座
　　　　　　 http://www.tup.com.cn　　邮　　　编：100084
　　　　　　 c-service@tup.tsinghua.edu.cn
　　　　　　 社 总 机：010-62770175　　邮购热线：010-62786544
　　　　　　 投稿咨询：010-62772015　　客户服务：010-62776969
印　装　者：北京地大彩印厂
经　　销：全国新华书店
开　　本：174×220　　**印　张**：4⅓　　**字　数**：139 千字
版　　次：2007 年 6 月第 1 版　　**印　次**：2007 年 6 月第 1 次印刷
印　　数：1～3000
定　　价：35.00 元